FEATHER REPORTS

Also by Derwent May and published by Robson Books

The New Times Nature Diary

FEATHER REPORTS

A Chronicle of Bird Life
from the Pages of *The Times*

DERWENT MAY

illustrated by Robin Jacques

Robson Books

This edition published in paperback in Great Britain in 1999 by Robson Books

First published in Great Britain in 1996 by Robson Books Ltd

British Library Cataloguing in Publication Data
A catalogue record for this title is available from the British Library

ISBN 1 86105 245 6

Designed by Harold King

Printed in Great Britain by
WBC Book Manufacturers, Bridgend, Mid Glam.

INTRODUCTION

B irds have haunted me since I was a boy. I do not know exactly what it is that still makes me look up every time I hear a starling singing or see a winged shadow cross my path, but I always feel the same faint thrill. And I feel a much more powerful thrill when I see a willow warbler taking a feather down to a clump of grass, and go across to find its half-built nest there, or when I hear a slightly peculiar nuthatch calling in a tree, track it down with my field-glasses and realize it is a wryneck – once a common bird, known as the 'cuckoo's mate', and now a rare one.

I think the pleasure is connected with their freedom from man. Endowed with that marvellous instrument of freedom, a pair of wings, most of them live their lives among men – whether in town or countryside – yet supremely indifferent to them. Only when people frighten them or when they can exploit men do they deign to take any notice. They divide the land up for their own purposes, and sing and mate and breed there; estate agents and high-taxing councils can gnash their teeth in vain.

There is also the beautiful economy of their lives. They do not plan, or even take thought, yet every swift, easy movement they make serves a purpose, contributing to their survival or the survival of their offspring. They live wonderfully elaborate lives just in order to live. They may not think as we do – but do they *feel* anything similar to us?

We do not know – but I find myself echoing the poet William Wordsworth's conviction, when contemplating the lambs playing and the birds singing:

> I must think, do all I can,
> That there was pleasure there.

Of course, some birds have suffered a serious drop in numbers in the last few decades, mainly due to the use by farmers of pesticides and herbicides, and the loss of suitable habitat. This is a change that we must try hard, and by every means, to reverse. However, I have concentrated here on the pleasure that is to be had from watching birds.

Feather Report has appeared as a regular weekly feature in *The Times* since the end of 1992. This selection of the articles is arranged month by month, and they are presented here almost exactly as they were written. I have tried to give a fresh and vivid account of the changing scenes of bird life through the year, as I have been observing them all my life – and still am.

The illustrations are by the late Robin Jacques, and all of them originally accompanied the articles in *The Times*. They appear here not only for their beauty and delicacy, but also as an act of homage to this fine artist. My thanks to the Editor of *The Times* for permission to reprint the articles and the drawings.

Derwent May

JANUARY

This morning I went bird-watching in the mist. A small silver sun occasionally gleamed in the sky and faded again. Fifteen yards away, the trees were obscure shapes. By the river towpath I was following, water-drops glinted on the dead rosettes of hogweed and wild angelica like a second, dream flowering. Underfoot, the fallen willow leaves were dark purple and silver-grey, like fish that had leaped out of the water and landed on the bank.

And birds? Well, at first it was a matter of ears. Birds are not much troubled by mist or rain, and soon a song-thrush's voice came ringing out of the mist, a double note repeated three times, then a triple note – followed by a collapse into a sort of scratchy babble, until the clear notes suddenly broke through again.

There was a sound like an oar creaking in a rowlock – but it was on the woodland side, not the river side. That was a foraging magpie. Then a great tit started chiming – 'Peter, Peter, Peter'. I could faintly hear another answering in the distance.

From over the river there came a sweeping 'chissick, chissick' – now, was that a pied wagtail or a grey wagtail looping away unseen? A pied wagtail, I thought – the calls of the two species are very similar, but the grey wagtail's is more of a slurred single note.

And then, I saw my first bird of the morning – one that is normally rather elusive. In the silence and the mist, it must have been as slow to notice me as I had been to notice it. On a willow trunk a few yards in front of me, a tree-creeper was making its way upwards with tiny jumps. For a moment, I had a very clear view of its gleaming white underside, its speckled brown back, its white eyestripe and its curved bill like a large caraway seed. It had a clear view of me too, and dropped from the trunk and flitted off into the mist.

There was a lake on the far side of the river, and the voice of a lapwing penetrated the air. It must be feeding out on a mud spit, I thought, but why was it calling? Was a gull watching it, and trying to snatch any morsel it picked up? As if in confirmation, I heard the wild screech of a black-headed gull.

I crossed a bridge and from the grass on the other side three moorhens stalked away. They jerked up their tails to show the white patches on either side as though they were putting on their rear lights for visibility. Mallards were cackling by the reeds at the lake's edge, but did not move: I watched them quarrelling and dabbling, then noticed a pheasant just by them in the weeds on the land.

After that I had to go back to my ears. The rest of the lake was totally hidden. Yet there were birds out there: a wigeon whistled, teal were making their liquid purring sounds and suddenly there was the shrill whinnying of a little grebe. The mist was thickening still more and it was time to turn back. But it had been a good morning's bird-hearing.

One of the most spectacular assemblies of birds to be seen at the moment is on the Ouse Washes, on the Cambridgeshire–Norfolk border. More than 4,000 wild swans are wintering on this flooded plain between the two great drainage canals of the Fens – the Old Bedford and the Hundred Foot rivers.

Over the water and the fields around, the sky is filled all day with the white wings of swans. There are three species present: about 3,500 Bewick's swans from the Russian tundra, 700 whooper swans mainly from Iceland, and a number of British mute swans.

Jacques

Teal

The deep, siren-like note made by the mute swans' wings as they fly can be heard up to a mile away. The northern swans fly more quietly, but the whoopers trumpet as they go: their brassy double cry always sounds to me like an Olympian cuckoo-call. The Bewick's swans also honk in the air, but their more characteristic note is a musical babble as they float on the water together.

The mute swans are easily picked out by their orange beaks. Both of the visiting species have black and yellow beaks, but the two species are not difficult to distinguish. The whooper swans are the same size as mute swans, and noticeably larger than the neat, rather 'goosey' Bewick's. The whoopers also have distinctly more yellow at the base of their beak than the Bewick's.

They can all be watched at close quarters from a huge, glass-fronted hide built at Welney by the Wildfowl and Wetlands Trust, which owns a large stretch of the Washes and has managed its waters so as to make it an attractive refuge for the wild swans.

Observers have discovered that the beak markings, especially of the Bewick's swans, differ considerably from bird to bird. Many of the swans return each year, and most of these are recognized as individuals by the Welney watchers. They have been given names such as Kon and Tiki or Swan and Vesta – since the pairs generally stay together for the whole of their lives. Visitors to the hide find a beak chart there which enables them to pick out the individual birds.

The swans are out in the arable fields for much of the day. It can be very bleak in mid-winter, but they find plenty of potatoes left by the harvesters, and particularly like them if they have been frozen and turned soft.

There is little other bird life in these fields, but along the rivers there are bushes and trees for small birds to shelter in, and occasionally a sparrow-hawk or even a wintering merlin sweeps along the banks.

The swans are fed twice a day by the Trust in the lagoon in front of the hide. They are thrown small quantities of waste potatoes and grain from a wheelbarrow. The first feed is by daylight at 3.30pm. There is a bigger feed, under floodlights, at 6.30pm, when all the swans have come back to roost.

It is amazing – even slightly dismaying – to see all these rare, wild creatures hustling each other to get at the food, unaware of their human audience.

Whooper Swan

The many ducks on the lagoon also join in, the pochards and the black-and-white tufted ducks, in particular, darting in and out, dodging the swans' beaks and diving for food as it goes under. Shyer ducks, such as pintails and shovelers, join in on the edge.

The Bewicks will be the first to leave, at the end of February – they have a long way to go, almost 2,500 miles, to their remote breeding grounds around the Kara Sea in Russia. The whoopers leave a month or so later. By spring, as the waters go down and the Washes revert to swampy grazing land, other birds, such as yellow wagtails, reed and sedge warblers, redshanks, and even black-tailed godwits, will take over.

The feeds are open to the public. In the afternoon you can go without booking but, for the floodlit feed, it is necessary to book in advance from the Wildfowl and Wetlands Trust at Welney in Cambridgeshire. It is also possible to stay overnight in the trust's Wigeon House, next door. That is the best thing to do, so that under the broad skies of the Fens you can watch the swans' short wintry day pass hour by hour.

Birds do not help each other much. Adult birds feed their young, and some male birds feed their mates on the nest – but the general rule is 'Every bird for itself'. The pied wagtail is very unusual in that some of the males have a servant in winter.

The pied or water wagtail is a little black-and-white bird with a long tail that bounces up and down all the time. It feeds on lawns and roads and roof-tops, as well as at the water's edge, where it will sometimes wade in. Many males guard a territory in winter, particularly along rivers, where each bird patrols his own stretch of bank looking for washed-up food.

However, it is sometimes hard to keep intruders out of the territory, and quite often the owner will allow a less dominant bird – a female, or a first-winter male – to live in the territory with him. It helps him drive intruders out, and is allowed to pick up any food surplus to the owner's requirements. In ornithological jargon, it is a satellite.

The pied wagtail has other interesting territorial habits. Its favourite food is the midges that swarm on pats of cow-dung, and in a field with many cows there may be quite a gathering of the birds. However, in the sunshine of the middle of the day, when the midges are swarming energetically, each of the pied wagtails will guard its own pat, as though it were its own table in a restaurant. In the cool of the evening, when the midges have gone, the birds abandon their miniature territories, and flock together to share the search for food.

The conversion of so many farms to unmixed arable land in eastern England has led to a drop in the number of pied wagtails there. It is not only the reduction in the number of cattle, but also the disappearance of farm ponds that has affected them.

However, they have increased in Wales and north-west England, and are perhaps more birds of the upland than they used to be. You find them nesting in stone walls in Scotland and the Lake District, as well as in all sorts of bizarre holes, like the glove-pockets of abandoned cars.

On the roads, they often pick up the insects hit by cars, as well as caterpillars that fall off overhanging trees. They run at their prey, giving a particularly vigorous wag of their tail at the end of each sprint.

They have a brisk, babbling song, heard in the spring and again briefly in the autumn, while their regular call-note is quite distinctive, a loud 'chissick'. They have the most undulating flight of all the British birds – and it is always a good moment for me when one comes bouncing through the air, making that call with each dip-and-rise, and settles with a flourish of its tail on the garage roof.

Over the brow of a sugar-beet field comes a sinister shape. It is only a few feet above the crop, and has long, upturned wings, with the tips of the fathers spread like a hand made of daggers. It takes a few flaps, then glides again.

When it sees you, it turns away with some more powerful wing-flaps, and now you can see that it is a dark-brown bird, heavily built, with a pale rump. It is a hen harrier. If you had been a small bird sheltering in the beet, it would have plunged down and carried you off.

Harriers always hunt in this way, flying low, looming up

suddenly, and swooping. They like to hunt in the large open spaces, and go up and down quartering the land. In the winter, you find them mostly near the coast, especially along the east coast, but they may turn up anywhere on lonely landscapes.

The brown birds are females. They are seen more often at this time of year than the males, which are smaller, and silvery-grey with inky wing-tips. At night they gather to roost in reed-beds or in long, rough grass, but at dawn they each return to their own hunting lands, where they work alone.

I have just been in Flevoland in Holland, driving through fields that were sea-bed only ten years ago. Hen harriers have flourished in this flat, empty countryside, and have grown much tamer than the few we see in Britain.

They were sitting on telegraph poles and the tops of roadside trees outside Lelystad, the new town of the polders, which has adopted the harrier as its symbol. The Dutch name for the harrier translates as 'chicken-thief', but they are rarely raiders of farmyards now.

It was very windy on the polders, and as the harriers peeled away from their perches, they demonstrated plainly their mastery of the air.

In summer, hen harriers go up to the Scottish moors to breed. There are also a small number nesting on the mountains of Wales and north-west England. There they give spectacular flying displays. The courting males soar into the sky, twist and plummet down, sometimes turning from side to side as they fall. They will even loop the loop.

One of the finest of all bird sights is a flock of wild geese passing overhead. They fly in arrowhead formation or in a slanting line, their long necks stretched out, and their voices ringing through the sky like a peal of bells or a pack of baying hounds.

There are three kinds of grey geese that come to Britain in large numbers in the winter – the pink-footed, the white-fronted and the greylag. They all have much the same way of life. They spend the night on sandbanks out in an estuary, or just offshore on a loch or a reservoir, and at dawn they stream away to feed in the fields. This dawn flight is best known to the wildfowlers, who take up their position in the darkness in a reedy dyke or behind a sea-wall, and have their brief moment of joy and slaughter as the geese sweep above them.

At sunset the geese return to the water (that is one reason why there are so may lurid sunsets in Peter Scott's paintings). In strong moonlight, they will make another night foray into the fields. They have a great appetite for grain and grass, potatoes and swedes – but they leave plenty of manure on the fields in return.

The north of Scotland is the place to see the greylag flocks. About 100,000 of them come down from Iceland to winter there. They are the largest of the three species, and are the ancestors of our farmyard geese, which they closely resemble – except that they run rather than waddle. In the air, their silvery-grey forewings pick them out. Some greylags also nest in the Hebrides. As you arrive on the ferry at Lochmaddy in North Uist in midsummer, you can see them sitting on a grassy harbour knoll.

The other two species are just winter visitors. The pinkfeet come from Greenland and Iceland, and inhabit the great coastal fields of southern Scotland and northern England. Large numbers of them roost on the Solway.

It is not easy to get close to them – you cross the brow of a field, and see a vast cloud of them rise from the far horizon, with high-pitched, penetrating cries. If you manage to get a good view, the contrast between their dark head and neck and their lighter back is noticeable. You may even get a glimpse of their pink feet.

The white-fronts come from Russian Siberia, and are best found in the waterlogged grassfields round the Severn. They can easily be watched from the hides at the Wildfowl and Wetlands Trust reserve at Slimbridge in Gloucestershire, which was founded by Peter Scott.

There are four or five thousand at Slimbridge each winter, and they move around as the floods move, but there is usually a flock somewhere in sight. Most of them have their heads down as they nibble and tug at the blades of grass – but there are always a few looking out for danger. Their name refers to the white patch at the base of their beak.

All these wild geese go back north in the spring – but the white-fronts are canny. Flying to Western Europe in the autumn, they go straight over Sweden. But in spring it is still very cold in the Baltic, so now they head east, stopping to feed all across Europe, and only turn north when they reach the Moscow longitude. They arrive fat and raring to breed at their Arctic summer home.

A walk on the clifftops of the English Channel has its winter pleasures. Out to sea, wailing laughter comes from the swirl of herring gulls, and beyond them, from time to time, one or two gannets go by. They are enormous shining white birds, with black tips at the end of their long wings; sometimes passing low over the water, sometimes well above it. They glide, give a few powerful flaps, then glide again.

Occasionally you are lucky enough to see one dive for a fish. It climbs high above the water then turns and plunges straight down, its wings angled like the letter W. Water rises like a bush around it as it hits the surface and goes under. When it emerges, it may rest for a moment on the sea to swallow its fish, before beating heavily up into the air again and disappearing towards the horizon.

On a still day, as the air warms above the land, up-currents of cooler air start to rise from the sea in front of the cliffs. The gulls take advantage of them, soaring and circling without a movement of their wings.

Now a fulmar petrel joins them, immediately distinguishable because its wings are straight and stiff and the grey on its back extends to the end of its tail. Through the field-glasses you can also see its thick-hooked beak, with a curious nostril-tube above it, giving the beak a two-tiered look. Fulmars are the supreme gliders of the sea, and the new arrival hangs motionless in the up-current.

If there are no hostile gulls about, another bird may profit from the upsurge of air: a kestrel. It can hover in any air conditions, but here it has an especially easy ride, and a fine opportunity to look out for rock pigeons.

This is also an opportunity for the bird-watcher to study kestrel plumage from above – the male with its orange back and blue tail, the female a duller, reddish-brown with her tail barred. On the rocks below, some cormorants are sitting with the spray breaking round them. One perched higher up has its wings spread out to dry, for cormorants' feathers are not very waterproof, even though they spend much of their life under water, swimming in pursuit of fish. When they fly off with their long necks stretched out, they look like black geese.

One's eyes are drawn constantly to the sea, but there is life on the clifftops, too. From a gorse bush in a gully comes a sharp note like two pebbles from the beach below being struck against each other. Then a small but very brightly coloured bird flies up to the top spray. It has a black head, a white collar and an orange breast, and it repeatedly twitches its wings and flicks its tail.

It is a male stonechat, a bird that particularly favours the scrubby edges of southern cliffs. Almost certainly it has a more plain-looking mate somewhere in the gorse patch, and they were probably feeding together on the ground when you came along. Handsome though it already is, it will look even finer in a month or two, when the brownish edges of its back feathers have been worn away, and its upper parts will look as shiny black as its head. The pair will nest deep down among the gorse prickles.

A few linnets fly by, with a kind of swishing twitter. One of them also lands on the top stem of a gorse bush, and sways there, looking keenly around, still twittering. This is another male bird, distinguished from its mate by the pale pink glow on its breast and its pink forehead. The pink will turn to a

Stonechat

deeper red as spring advances, and its lazy, twanging song will be heard more and more.

In the dead bracken by the side of the path there is sound and movement now. An unseen wren bursts into loud song for a moment, and then a very small greenish bird flits from one feathery brown frond to another. It must be a goldcrest or a firecrest. But which?

A firecrest is more likely, even though it is a much less common bird in Britain, because wintering firecrests often settle in places like this. Goldcrests are more likely to stay around the conifer trees in which they breed.

The greenish tint also suggests a firecrest – but the bird has vanished. Suddenly it comes out again, and in that moment you see not only the brilliant yellow line along the top of the head but also – crucial for identification – the clear white eye-stripe, with black lines above and below it. The goldcrest lacks that white eyestripe so a firecrest it is, probably one that came over from the Continent in October.

What else on the clifftop on this late January day? A meadow pipit goes up from the grass with a thin call, rising jerkily into the sky as though it were climbing a flight of stairs.

Then, high up somewhere, a skylark starts singing; a song that goes on and on, its pitch rising and falling. You pick it out, a tiny shape fluttering sturdily into the growing wind; then it stops and drops to the ground. You stand still, listening intently, but the land has gone silent again. You are left with only the rumbling and roar of the waves and the distant, wind-broken cries of the seagulls.

FEBRUARY

Early in February, in every wood and garden, new maps are being drawn: chaffinches are staking out their territories around a fruit tree to nest in, blackbirds doing the same round a thick hedge, great tits round a suitable hole or nesting-box. Song-thrushes, robins and wrens have already marked out their territories during the winter.

None of these species has the least interest in any of the other species. For example, blackbirds want only to keep other blackbirds out of their territories, great tits to keep out other great tits. So all these territories are superimposed on each other. An avian estate agent would have a terrible time making a plan of your garden and those around it. There might be nine or ten different boundaries to be drawn in different coloured inks, all criss-crossing each other at innumerable points. But as long as the inhabitants can keep out rivals of the same species, they all live happily together on the same plot.

How clear and firm these territorial boundaries are is not so easy to say. When David Lack wrote his marvellous book *The Life of the Robin* in the late 1930s, he drew precise maps of a set of adjacent robin territories. He had colour-ringed the robins and noted the points where they challenged or fought each other, and he drew boundaries linking up those points.

Now it would generally be considered that the robins and other territorial birds have a much looser idea of how much land they consider to be theirs, and one that changes as the spring goes on. What remains constant, however, is the way most species of small birds proclaim their ownership – which is by their song.

Birdsong may have other uses, especially that of attracting a mate, but its main function is to warn off other birds. The millions of male wrens that have carved up Britain according to their needs, and are now going higher into the trees to sing their loud and brilliant song, are really shouting 'Keep out!' to other wrens.

An experiment carried out some years ago with great tits in an Oxfordshire wood demonstrated beautifully this use of song. Some great tits were trapped and removed from their territories. The result was that others from rather poorer breeding areas – less food, more cats – moved in.

Then some more great tits were removed, but now loudspeakers giving forth the song of the great tit were set up in their territories. This time no great tits tried to take over the vacant lots.

Birds do battle on the boundaries, though usually without much actual fighting. You often see two robins facing each other in adjacent hawthorn trees on a roadside, both singing in a shrill, strained way, with their bodies drawn up to show the maximum amount of red breast to their antagonist. The coloured feathers add to the impact of the song.

Why exactly birds need territories is unresolved, but it seems clear that the males want to prevent other males from impregnating their mate, and that the pair want some kind of guaranteed food supply for their nestlings.

Meanwhile, the dawn chorus of song is just beginning and will swell over the next two or three months. Why do birds sing so much at dawn? The answer here seems to be that it is still too dark to find food, but not too dark to do a bit of territory-proclaiming. Birds do not want to waste time.

But pity the poor avian estate agent when we get to April.

Then the woods will be flooded with summer visitors – willow warblers, chiffchaffs, blackcaps, garden warblers – all eager to impose their territorial maps on top of all the others. It will be chaos for the surveyor. But the birds themselves will not notice that there is any problem at all.

‘It's just a house sparrow’ – can there be a bird-watcher who hasn't sometimes said that? But of late, as some of the common birds have grown scarcer, I think many people have been looking at sparrows with a more appreciative eye.

House sparrows are certainly a remarkable species. They are what the zoologists call ‘commensals’ – in other words, they feed ‘at the same table’ as humans. They probably evolved as eaters of grass seeds on the savannahs, and even now they are commoner on the dry east side of England than they are in the wet west. But ever since we started cultivating

House Sparrow

the fields, they have lived with us, feeding on grain and nesting under our eaves.

They repay a close look as they fly up on to a wall and perch there for a moment. I sometimes think of the male as a sort of black and brown great tit, with its cap and bib and white wing-bar. As a seed-eater, it has a stouter beak than the tits, but it is just as lively, for ever looking round and restlessly flicking its tail. The female is duller – and both are different from the tree sparrows, a patchily distributed rural species in which both sexes have a chestnut cap and a distinctive dark cheek-mark. As for the bird called a 'hedge sparrow', that is not a sparrow at all, but a thin-billed insect-hunter that scuttles under the bushes on pink feet, and is now generally called by its old name of dunnock.

In winter, towards dusk, you often hear a tremendous chattering coming from the ivy. That is the young house sparrows gathering for the night. The birds that bred last year prefer to roost in the holes and crevices where they had their nests.

They breed communally, and this leads them into various tricks. Male sparrows will kill the young birds in another sparrow's nest, and try to mate with the bereaved mother. A female will often lay some eggs in another sparrow's nest as well as its own. If it is lucky, the other female will bring up these additional young. Perhaps cuckoos began in this way, then moved on to laying their eggs in the nests of other species.

By living with man, house sparrows have learnt to feed on many other things besides grain – but when the corn is getting ripe they go down to the fields in flocks. Young and old set off together, and it is rather like a summer holiday. They fly up and down constantly between the hedges and the wheat, never going too far out into the field but having a tremendous feast.

In February and March they are destructive (from a human point of view) in another way. They attack the yellow crocus flowers and scatter the petals over the grass in what seems like wanton destruction. In fact, it is now thought that they are getting at the crocus stigmas. These contain saffron – a source of Vitamin A.

Yes – when a sparrow falls, a lot falls with it.

Skylarks are singing again over the fields. The song trickles down from the sky, unbroken, constantly changing – though as you listen, you notice recurrent phrases, the high soprano notes often followed by a little burst of deep contralto. They will sing for three minutes at a time, sometimes five. They hover on one spot, or move slowly forward into the wind. When they come down, they sweep round in a wide circle, then suddenly plummet. After landing they stand out like pale stones among the first green shoots of winter corn.

What are they doing up there? Actually, they are not interested in the sky – what concerns them is the ground beneath. Up in the air they are marking out invisible boundaries to the earthly plot where in summer they will nest and get much of their food. Down below, if another skylark tries to enter that plot, the owner will warn it off, the crest on his head lifted in defiance. They will even fight briefly.

All this activity is in anticipation of the birds' needs in the longer, warmer days. For the present, the song is heard mainly in the mornings. Later in the day, the skylarks will flock up again to look for food. They appear quite different when they fly near the ground from when they are hovering overhead. They have a rather hesitant, fluttering wing beat –

and when a flock rises together, the birds waver in all directions, as if some wind from the centre of the flock was blowing them all about.

Some of these flocking birds will never sing here. They are winter immigrants from the Continent, who will be moving back home from March onwards and will take up their territories in Germany or further north. But all the skylarks have the same distinctive flight call, a rippling 'chirrup' that has been one of the typical sounds of our farmland since the forests were first cut down.

However, new farming practices have conspired against the skylark in recent years. The tendency to plant corn in autumn rather than spring means that the winter stubble-fields where skylarks traditionally fed have largely disappeared. It also means that the barley seed that they would turn to in February is gone. Luckily, they also feed on clover and the leaves of kale and beet.

However, their breeding has also been affected. In many fields the corn is now too high in spring to provide a suitable nesting place for them.

'Set-aside' promised to help them with both food and nesting-sites, but for several years farmers were obliged to cut down the weeds on any set-aside land early in the summer, with much resultant destruction of nests.

That is no longer necessary, and many farmers are trying to give skylarks a better chance. They could soon be singing all over the heavens again.

St Valentine's Day is traditionally the day when birds choose their mates for the year, and it is true that if you go around the countryside in mid-February you are very conscious of birds being about in pairs.

I have just been out in some Surrey woodland. It has been a warm, dry day and the treetops were full of noisy nuthatches. Some were making that breathy twitter, like a hammer glancing off a piece of metal, that you hear all the year round; others were giving their long, clear spring whistles. I quickly picked one out walking head downwards on a dead branch at the top of an oak. It was feeding, but it was also looking into holes.

Suddenly another came buzzing through the air and landed by it, and the two of them went up and down the dead wood together. They were obviously a pair thinking about where they might make their nest later on. They nest in large holes, plastering

Jacques

Nuthatch

up most of the entrance with mud, and a female choosing her mate will need to be sure that he has suitable holes in his territory. Their blue backs stood out very brightly against the pale, barkless wood.

After that it was all pairs. One jay started screaming in a tree, and another flew in and screamed with it. I did not think they were screaming at me, and I was soon proved right – a sparrow-hawk which they must have already spotted flapped overhead and glided away. I say 'screamed', which is how that harsh cry of the jay is usually described, but I have found a more precise comparison. I recently heard a man blowing his nose in a very loud, determined way, and I thought 'That sound seems familiar'. Then I realized it was exactly like a jay's call.

The next pair were mistle-thrushes, very symmetrically arranged. A large garden with two tall cypresses in it abutted on the wood, and the birds were sitting side by side, one on the top of each tree, warming their breasts in the mid-morning sun, and churring gently. In that light their spotted breasts looked yellow.

Then I found a lone bird, and we played a game together. I was crossing a more open piece of sandy ground with just a few trees on it, and a green woodpecker flew up from the grass, and settled behind the trunk of one of the trees. I approached slowly, and off it went and did the same on the next tree and then the next. It obviously did not want to go far – I imagine it had found some well-stocked anthills. So I circled round and advanced from the opposite direction. This time it flew back and landed on the grass again.

In the same low sunshine I had an unusually good view of its back, the colour of olive moss, the brilliant red top of its head, and its little black moustache. The fact that the moustache did not have a red centre meant that it was a female. Woodpeckers pair later in the year than many species, and this was obviously one who had not yet made up her mind.

Back in the wood, pairs of starlings were sitting together, with each male producing clicks and whirrings and whistles from his wide-open beak, and waving his wings aggressively at other starlings which passed. A flock of jackdaws circled overhead with clacking cries; then they came tumbling down into the branches where they too disposed themselves in intimate-looking pairs. As I left the wood, there was a screech even more startling than a jay's, and a pair of ring-tailed parakeets shot overhead, their long tails trailing.

St Valentine was doing his stuff. In fact, there is a value in this tendency of birds to form pairs a good couple of months before they mate and breed. In the winter, it is every bird for him or herself. But now the pairs have a kind of quiet, sexless honeymoon in which they can become familiar with each other. Paired birds are far more unfaithful to each other than was once supposed. But the bond that they forge in these early spring days does seem to contribute to keeping them together in the busy months of breeding ahead.

In mid-February, if the weather is not too harsh, herons begin to return to their bulky nests in the tree-tops. A heronry is rather like a giants' rookery – yet the nests can easily be overlooked if they are in the middle of a dense copse, or if they are built in the high boughs of tall pines.

The males come back to the heronry first. They have a slow, heavy wing-beat when they are plodding across the skies in search of quiet river banks and ponds, but now they glide the last few yards into the trees. They stand on the old nests, or among the branches if they are first-time nesters; they turn the old nest-material over, or tug at the twigs around them, stretching out their long necks and using their dagger-like yellow bills.

Over the next few weeks, the females will come sailing in. When one approaches a male, there is an extraordinary greeting ceremony. The male sets up a wild, harsh honking, and the female answers with a vibrant cry. The male stretches himself to his full height, and points his straightened neck and his beak vertically at the sky. He is a striking sight with his blue-grey back and his long black crest hanging down the back of his head – quite unlike the hunched-up bird that one sees waiting beside a pool for a fish. Then the two birds clatter their beaks at each other. Slowly, with frequent repetitions of this tree-top ceremony, the bond becomes established.

At a later stage, before actual mating, the male will offer sticks to the female, and nest-building or repairs will fill much of their days. Around this time, too, the herons often soar and glide with tilting wings in the air above the trees.

By March, each pair will have four or five large, light blue eggs in their nest, and the incubating bird will be almost hidden behind its ramparts.

Heronries may contain large numbers of birds, or have only two or three nests in them. But by the middle of February even the smallest heronry is a noisy place, with greeting cries, angry quarrelling outbursts, and other snoring and retching sounds coming from the breeding birds. Sometimes you can see the herons powdering themselves. They have one large and two smaller patches of 'powder-down' on their underparts – very fine, friable feathers that continually turn to dust at the tip. The herons dip their beaks into this dust and rub it over their bodies. It cleans the feathers and helps to waterproof them.

By mid-May, when many other species are just beginning to nest, the young herons will be reaching full-size and preparing to fend for themselves. Why does the heron nest so early? It is thought that the herons' breeding season is connected with the speed and intensity with which herons have to feed their large young. If the eggs hatch in March or early April, their parents are likely to find the marshes and lakes free of ice, and fish, frogs and voles already plentiful. But if they left their breeding much later, they would find the waterside vegetation growing up rapidly, and hunting would be a distinctly longer and more difficult job, as their prey would be less visible.

Of course, there can often be hard weather still to come in February, and that delays everything. Survival is the first demand on a bird, and herons do not find it easy when the lakes and pools are frozen. Some go down to the sea, some risk a visit at dawn to city rivers; but there is usually a high death-rate from starvation in a bad winter. Even so, many birds always get through it, and the heronry returns to life, albeit in somewhat depleted strength.

The population will probably never get much larger, however mild our winters. Herons need undisturbed solitude for catching fish, and they space themselves out across the countryside in the comparatively small number of places where they can find it.

So herons will not swarm on the river banks like Canada geese. But on a day out in the country there is always a good chance of seeing one of these powerful wanderers – in the spring sunshine, foraging for its nestlings by a riverside miles from the heronry, or on a bleak winter's day beating through the sky on its solitary way from reed-bed to reservoir.

Are magpies monsters? Many people think so. When I wrote an article once saying that their attacks on eggs and nestlings had no serious effect on the population of small songbirds, I received some anguished letters of protest. 'For the past few years,' wrote one correspondent, 'I have watched helplessly as magpies have raided nests, and the frantic parent birds have tried to protect them . . . . You are overlooking a massive change.'

Magpies certainly do feed on other birds' eggs and nestlings when they can find them, mainly in spring and early summer, but a series of censuses by the British Trust for Ornithology, covering magpies and eight species of common songbirds, show that there is no correlation between an increase in magpies and a decline in small birds. On the contrary, where the magpie population has increased, the

Magpie

number of small birds has also increased – both benefiting, perhaps, from some common factor, such as cover.

Magpies have certainly become more numerous since the late 1940s, chiefly due to the diminished population of gamekeepers. But on the evidence, there is no reasonable case for shooting them.

Of course, if one has had the luck to find a robin's nest behind the bark of a tree in the garden, it is sickening to see a magpie cackling and gulping down the eggs. The BTO suggests various measures of protection against such local ravages. A piece of wire netting, with holes big enough for the parents to go through, can be attached above a nest, and that will put magpies off. Doors of little-used sheds can be left open so that blackbirds can nest on shelves and window-ledges: magpies will not venture in. Cats do far more harm – but I do not recommend shooting those, either.

I am glad that magpies are so abundant. They are very beautiful birds when the light catches them the right way – not just black and white, but with a purple-blue gloss on their heads and backs, blue and green lights on their wings, and even a red gleam in the tail.

Their movements are wonderfully varied. They stalk about with their long tails lifted or move away in long, bounding hops. They slip deftly among branches and twigs, raising and dropping and fanning their tails for balance. They are rather comic in the air, flying heavily with desperately fast flaps, or finding their tails blown over their heads by a following wind.

In early spring they behave in a particularly dramatic way. Young males try to claim territories, and when two males start quarrelling in a tree, other magpies come pouring in to take part. You can sometimes see 20 or 30 of them among the boughs, all chattering and many of them displaying, with white shoulders puffed out and head feathers raised in a crest.

They will soon start nesting, building large domes of earth and twigs in blackthorn hedges and small, thick trees, though two months may pass before the clutch of five or six mottled blue-green eggs is laid.

Especially in winter, they store food in holes in the ground. Earthworms are one of the main items of diet. They have also been known to attack cartons of eggs left by milkmen on doorsteps.

They have no natural enemies – apart from the great spotted cuckoo in the Mediterranean, which has adopted the magpie as its main victim, laying several eggs in one nest, and leaving the young cuckoos and magpies to fight it out among themselves.

L ate February is the time to have a close look at a long-tailed tit. The pairs are just beginning to leave the winter flocks, and start surveying bushes and hedges for possible nesting places. They are very tame when they do this. You hear their distinctive mutterings from inside a low cypress, peer through the branches, and there you see one a foot or two away.

Normally one thinks of them as little black and white birds – but now you can see that their lower back, their stomach, their flanks and part of their wings are suffused with pink.

The sexes are alike – except that later in the spring you can sometimes distinguish a female by her bent tail. This is the result of her sitting with it folded up for long hours in the domed nest.

The pair still go back at night to roost in the flock, and will continue to do so until they have finished the dome on their nest, when they will move there for the night. On cold nights they roost huddled together on a twig. First two birds settle, pressed together; then another squeezes between them, and so on until they are as tightly packed as they can be.

The winter flocks are usually families that stayed together after the summer, and the young birds in them have a curious way of finding mates. When there is some quarrel over territorial boundaries with another winter flock, the females slip over to the enemy side, and find a young male there. Then they stay in the adoptive flock until nesting-time comes.

Long-tailed tits are among the earliest nesters, and some will be starting at the beginning of March. They make a small platform of moss in a cypress or gorse or thick hawthorn bush, binding it down with spiders' webs. Then they build up the walls and the dome in the same way. Finally they line it with feathers, quite often as many as 1,500.

It is a long, hard job and after all that, when they lay their eggs in these conspicuous early nests, a jay often gets them. So they start all over again.

Even at this stage they retain some family feeling. It has been noticed in recent years that there are sometimes more than two adults feeding the nine or ten young birds in the nest.

What appears to happen is that brothers of the breeding male who have not found a mate help with his family. Even more remarkably, sisters who have lost their later-season nests come back to their brother, and help him too. All of them will stay together in next winter's flock.

At any time of year, to my mind, they are an absolutely delightful sight. When you see them flitting between two trees, like flying teaspoons, they look quite unbalanced. But when they are feeding in the tree-tops, swinging and swaying on the twigs, you realize that their long tail is working away for them, just like a tightrope walker's pole.

MARCH

April may be the cruellest month for poets, but March can often be the cruellest month for birds. It marks the moment when winter food supplies are almost exhausted, and spring food supplies have hardly begun. Harsh weather in March can turn the screw with fatal results.

Greenfinches are among the most vulnerable birds. Those that are managing all right are already making their wheezing spring call in the treetops, and will soon be singing. But for some of them survival is still touch-and-go.

In winter they feed in large, noisy flocks on grain and weed seeds from last summer's plants. Charlock seeds, the hooked seeds of burdock and even wild rosehips can all be found on the plant or on the ground until well into the new year. Grain is harder to find nowadays, because not much is left to be gleaned on the stubble fields after the combine harvesters have been over them.

After those food sources have come to an end, greenfinches can turn in early spring to the new seeds already ripening on dandelions, groundsel and chickweed. But bad weather can hold those flowers back – and every year, in the gap between the seasons, some greenfinches die of hunger or, in their enfeebled state, are caught by cats or sparrow-hawks.

Goldfinches are in the same position. Many of them leave Britain for France or Spain in the winter. But some stay here, feeding on the thistleheads and on teasel, and for them, too, last year's seeds may all have vanished before the dandelion clocks start blowing.

Great tits and blue tits have it a little easier. In the autumn, they often eat beech mast, and in the winter, with their small, thin beaks, they can dig out tiny insects in a way that is not natural to the stout-beaked finches. There are plenty of insects around in different forms all through the winter. Many moths lay their eggs on branches or twigs in the autumn, like the lichen-green moth with the splendid name *merveille du jour*, which lays its eggs on oak trees.

The eggs of another woodland moth, the oak eggar, hatch in autumn, but in this species the caterpillars hibernate on the trees. Innumerable moth chrysalids also lie in cracks in the bark waiting for the spring.

Tits can find all these, and can even cope well in snowy weather. There may be snow on the top of branches, but they can hang beneath them and search the undersides. What really makes their life difficult is severe frost. When ice locks the branches in a coat of glass, they are defeated.

Blackbirds and song-thrushes have different feeding problems. They eat fruit and berries in the autumn and early winter. The song-thrushes hop about delicately under the fruit trees, the blackbirds squabble over the berries in the hawthorn hedges.

After Christmas, they are obliged to turn to earthworms. They can spot the worms' burrows where a dead leaf sticks out, and hear them moving under the earth. Roadsides are good places for them, because the rumbling of lorries brings worms to the surface.

This is also the chief time of the year for song-thrushes to find snails and crack their shells open on a stone. But in March, if the ground is frozen solid or buried under snow, blackbirds and thrushes have few other resources.

So this is the most important time of the year for keeping the bird tables well-stocked. Of course, birds will come for easy food at any time of the year – they're only avian, after all.

But from spring to early winter they really do not need much human help. When there is frost and snow – and even after the snow and frost have gone – March is the month to remember them. Even the wild winter thrushes, redwings and fieldfares may come to your garden.

Fieldfare

Over the fields there is a new sound: the call of the lapwings displaying. They are back from their winter wanderings, and the males are tumbling and diving over their territories. Birds of open spaces with no high perches

Lapwing

to sit on almost always sing and display in the sky; that is why the skylarks also sing high in the air.

Another common name for the lapwing is peewit, which is a good imitation of its call. The note is heard all the year round, but takes on a new character in these spring gyrations. The bird rises slowly from the ground on its curious, rounded wings, then climbs abruptly, calling with a long, plaintive 'pee-weet-weet'. Suddenly it lets itself fall, twisting, and even somersaulting, as it comes down, and calls again more sharply. As it falls, it is a swirl of black and white, for it is black above, and white beneath the inner wing and on the under-parts. Before it lands it straightens up and makes a low humming sound with its wings.

On the ground, in the sunshine, the bird shows why it has yet another name: the green plover, because it has a green sheen on the black back. Altogether it is a striking bird, with its long crest and its black gorget, standing erect in the field.

When it feeds, it tilts its whole body forward, revealing a patch of orange under its tail.

The sky display warns off other male lapwings and attracts a female. When a female lands in the territory, the male courts her by running towards her with head and neck stretched forward and the crest lowered. He also makes scrapes in the ground, pressing his chest into the earth and scratching with his feet. It is as though he were showing her their potential home together. Indeed, if they pair up, one of these scrapes will be chosen as the nest and lined with dry grass.

Lapwings are early breeders, and the four mottled eggs, arranged in the shape of a cross, may be laid before the end of March.

There are other plovers in some fields: golden plovers. But these are flocks of wintering birds waiting for warmer weather before they return to the moors to nest. They are hard to see on a ploughed field; sometimes you first detect them when one lifts a wing, showing its white under-side. Their dark backs are spangled with gold, and they stand very upright, with their rather square heads held high. They have large, soft eyes and a dainty bill. Their call is a single liquid whistle.

Plovers are members of the great wader family, and when golden plovers fly up they look more like typical waders than the floppy-winged lapwings. They cut through the air on sharp wings in close formation, then spread out as they glide in and land again.

Another new call in the meadows, or among lines of growing corn, is a loud 'chukka-chukka'. This is the spring call of the French, or red-legged, partridge, which is now more often seen than the common, or grey, partridge in some parts of the country. It is a larger bird than the ordinary partridge, but you need a good view to see its fine markings.

Apart from its red legs and beak, it has rich barring on the flanks, blue on the chest, a black border to its white throat and orange-brown upper parts. When alarmed, it is more inclined to run than the common partridge, which goes off on whirring wings.

With skylark song cascading from the sky, lapwings crying, yellowhammers singing in the hedges, partridges calling and lambs bleating, there is a lot to be heard in the fields as the spring equinox draws near.

Gannets are returning to the cliffs and rocky islets where they nest. All through the winter they have been far from home. The younger birds have been fishing in the warm seas off West Africa. The older ones have been out in the North Sea and the Atlantic, or drifting round European shores.

They are among our most spectacular birds. Just to see two or three flying across the horizon is an arresting sight. They are pure white, apart from yellowish heads and black wing tips, and they are almost 4ft long from the tip of their fierce bill to the end of their pointed tail. They glide smoothly over the waves, or pass by with majestic wing beats high above the water.

The younger birds look quite different from the adults. The juveniles are practically black, with white flecks. Slowly the black diminishes and the white areas grow – but it is five years before they are fully grown.

Best of all is to see gannets fishing. When they detect a shoal of fish under the water they rise slightly in the air, half-close their wings, and plunge like a harpoon into the sea. Their wings close tighter just before they enter the water, but they still raise a tremendous splash.

Air sacs under their feathers fill out as they dive, and cushion them against the impact of the water. The air sacs also bring them to the surface again before they need to breathe. They swallow whole the fish they have caught, and clumsily take to the air again.

Gannets are found only in small parties in the winter, but in the summer they are among the most intensively colonial of all birds. They nest on suitable cliff ledges in vast numbers, just out of range of each other's beaks. Around the north and west coasts of Britain there are about 150,000 breeding pairs – with 50,000 of those on the small St Kilda's island of Boreray. Another well-known breeding site is the Bass Rock in the Firth of Forth, which you can sail around in a boat from North Berwick.

By March the first males are back on the ledges, trying to attract passing females. Courtship involves much head-shaking and clattering together of beaks by the prospective pair, and it is followed by tender mutual preening as they settle down together.

However, when a female is away fishing, the male may at this early stage lure another female to his ledge, and when the first one comes back there will be a fierce fight between the two females.

It all sounds very human, but there is probably a biological advantage in the male's faithless behaviour. His first choice may well have gone fishing hundreds of miles away – and faced with the hazards of the sea may never return.

Later the pair get to know each other's voices. They take turns to incubate their solitary egg, and when the one who has been out feeding returns, it soars up the cliff face calling with a raucous cry. Gannets, herring gulls, fulmars and kittiwakes may be swirling about the ledges, but amidst all the din, the incubating bird recognizes its mate's call and prepares to greet it.

For centuries, gannet eggs and fat young gannets were taken for food by marauding humans hanging on ropes down the cliff face. It has been estimated that a million gannets have been taken from the Bass Rock alone in the last thousand years. Now they are protected by law, which may be why their numbers are slowly increasing.

Even if there is still fierce weather to come they will not be much troubled by it. They sit on their ledges, warm in their thick feathers, till a blizzard has passed. Then they drop off on to an air current, and are soon far away – lonely white hunters of the sea again.

The first summer migrants usually arrive back in Britain in mid-March. Here and there, on the downs or on a playing field, people will see a dapper grey bird flicking its tail and bobbing up and down as it looks for insects in the grass. When it flies off, going low over the ground, it will show a conspicuous white rump.

That white rump has given the bird its name, wheatear – which simply means 'white arse'. The word dates from a time when 'arse' was still in polite use – and the first half of the name has nothing to do with 'wheat' at all.

These wheatears are the first of hundreds of thousands that will be making their way up through Europe between the middle of March and May.

They winter in Africa, south of the Sahara, and come north in a leisurely fashion, starting early and stopping frequently. They even hold small territories on migration if they find a good stopover for a few days. Some will go up to the far north of Europe, and then either swing left for Greenland and Canada, or right for Siberia.

In this country, a certain number stay to nest on the downs, but most go on to the rocky hillsides of Wales and the north. They are birds that need large horizons – you will never see them in a garden, let alone a wood. They nest in rabbit burrows or in cracks in dry stone walls, and their blacks, greys and whites camouflage them well against such a background. At Dungeness, several pairs usually nest in the shingle in old ammunition boxes that have been specially planted there for them.

Few birds are so brisk and lively, and they are a constant pleasure to watch. The male has a short warbling song, like a rather creaky skylark, and often flies up from a rock and dances in the air to deliver it. Wheatears will also fly up and hover briefly just to look about them. Hunting for food, they repeatedly pause, then hop or run smartly forward. When they are alarmed, they fly up on to a boulder and make sharp cries, or a note like stones being knocked together. To dodge a hawk, they will dive into a rabbit hole.

They lay five or six pale blue eggs. Birds that nest in dark holes or hollows generally have white or blue eggs, because these are easier for the parents to see, and eggs hidden in holes do not need colour camouflage.

When migration begins again in the autumn, the slightly larger Greenland wheatears become quite common for a while in Britain. What is strange is that those birds which went off in spring in the direction of Canada, and those that went in the other direction to Siberia, both return to Europe, and only then turn south, back down the route they went up by. It would make far more sense for the first group to winter in Central America, and for the second group to winter in Southern Asia.

But they have not made this adaptation, even though it means that some of them have the longest migratory flight of any small bird in the world. That is the route their ancestors discovered in early evolutionary times – and that is the route that they stick to.

I have just heard my first chiffchaff. It is March 20 – a typical date. That sharp 'tink-tank' song, slowly and rhythmically repeated, carries a long way, and I had to walk a good 200 yards before I found the bird in a willow tree at the edge of a river. It was fluttering and darting among the twigs in pursuit of flies, but it kept on singing.

Was it a newly arrived migrant from the Mediterranean? No ornithologist could be sure. Most of the 600,000 pairs of chiffchaffs that breed in Britain every summer pass the winter on the Mediterranean coast, or just south of the Sahara, but a few remain here and survive the cold.

These hardy spirits do not sing in the winter, and are difficult to detect, but it is possible that they start singing here in spring just before the visitors arrive.

Anyway, the migrants will soon be pouring in and the treetops will be full of their song. There is just a week or two in which to see them easily among the branches before they are all half-hidden by the fresh, green leaves.

Chiffchaffs are small green birds, paler beneath and with a light stripe over the eye. They are very similar to their close relatives the willow warblers, which will be arriving in even greater numbers from early April onwards. Apart from the fact – not often very helpful to the bird-watcher – that the chiffchaff generally has black legs and the willow warbler has red legs, about the only thing that easily distinguishes the two species is their song.

This difference no doubt evolved so that the birds themselves should not get muddled and try to mate with the wrong species, but it is good news for us, too.

You cannot confuse the chiffchaff's chinking song with the willow warbler's long, trickling musical cadence which, a friend once told me, makes him think of a silk shawl slowly slipping off a woman's shoulders.

The male chiffchaffs take up their territories in woodland

that offers both tall trees for song posts and thick undergrowth, such as brambles, for their mates to nest in. They usually build their domed nests about a foot or two above the ground.

Willow warblers settle in birch woods and young conifer plantations, and build rather neater domed nests under tussocks of grass and low bramble shoots.

Chiffchaffs are less common than willow warblers in the north, though in Scotland they are often found in the policies – the parks and gardens laid out around a large country house. Willow warblers' songs can be heard in the summer ringing out from far away across the glens.

One difference I have noticed between the two species is that when they are nest building, the female chiffchaffs make their soft, warning call note – 'hweet' – whereas the female willow warblers are completely silent.

This makes it much easier to find chiffchaffs' nests at this early stage – if you hear one calling like this at the end of

Chiffchaff

April it will very likely have a stem of dry grass or a feather in its beak, and you can easily watch to see where it lands. A month or so later, when they are feeding the young, both species will be calling like this, or almost like it.

But that is a story to come back to on a day in June. We have all the spring to live through before then.

By the end of March the great spring migration is thoroughly under way. Chiffchaffs and sand martins have been arriving in Britain for a week or more and literally millions of other summer visitors – swallows, willow warblers, tree pipits, quail – are coming up through Africa and southern Europe in their wake. A good many migrants probably cross the equator on the spring equinox itself – exchanging the long days of the southern hemisphere for the long days of the northern at precisely the right moment.

Among these arrivals there are a few that, though not rare, are scarce enough to provide a special thrill. They are all birds that one might encounter, with no special effort and a bit of luck, on a country walk.

One species that is always startling is the black tern. Terns, like gulls, seem such quintessentially white birds that when you find two or three black terns hawking over a lake in April, you feel you have stepped through the mirror into a world of opposites. They have black heads and bodies, and dark grey under-wings; otherwise they are just like the more familiar terns, patrolling over the water with long wings and forked tails. Occasionally they arrive in hundreds on an east wind, and the sky over a gravel pit is full of dark shapes like devils.

In the early nineteenth century they used to nest quite commonly in southern England, but now only an occasional pair makes an attempt to breed on the Ouse Washes. Most of them go on to northern Europe.

Garganeys often arrive at the end of March. They are small ducks, like teal, and the drake has a dashing white eyestripe that identifies it immediately. When they stop to feed on migration, they lurk at the edge of lakes. A few stay to nest in rushy marshes and water meadows – the more so when there is plenty of lying water after a winter of floods. When they stay to nest they are often detected by their curious crackling note coming from the low reeds.

Lakes also attract one of the most spectacular of migrants: the osprey. With protection from humans, this great fish-hawk has made a striking comeback as a breeding bird in the Scottish Highlands, and now about 60 pairs nest each year in lochside pines.

From the end of March onwards they can turn up anywhere in the South or the Midlands; they are often seen on Rutland Water. They have gleaming white heads and bodies, and dark, angled wings: they fly slowly over the surface of the water, and dive dramatically into it for food, feet first. They have unusual feet, adapted for catching fish, with long bent talons and spines on the soles. If their dive is successful, they fly to a lakeside tree to eat the fish, holding it head forward as a further touch of streamlining.

Cattle egrets, or buff-backed herons, have been appearing here in the spring more often in recent years. They are small white herons, with golden-brown plumes on their back in their summer plumage. On the Continent, they are often seen striding about on their long, red legs around the legs of cows, but here they are more likely to be found at the water's edge. A few little egrets, which are taller with long white plumes on the head and back, are nowadays to be seen throughout the winter.

I must not omit the hoopoe, which is sometimes seen

walking about tamely on a lawn or a garden path. It is unmistakable, with its pink body, its pink crest tipped with black, and its barred black-and-white wings. Its name comes from its bizarre song – a repeated 'hoop-hoop' that at a little distance sounds just like a dog going 'woof-woof'.

APRIL

When I was a schoolboy I devised a proverb: 'This year's nests are never found till next.' Every winter, when the last leaves had blown off the hedges, I was astonished at how many wrecked, rubbish-filled nests were revealed of which I had had no inkling the previous summer.

Early spring is the time to find nests, when the hedges have only the first dusting of green on them, and one can still see any dark concentration of matter silhouetted against the sky. Bird-watchers have become rather puritanical in recent years; some think it a crime to search for nests, or even to take a brief look if you stumble across one. They believe that any action that jeopardizes the birds' breeding success is unethical.

A clutch of brightly coloured eggs in a newly built nest is one of the most delightful sights in nature, and I usually do take a brief, careful look if I find one. However, one should not scare an incubating bird off the eggs – although they almost invariably come back as soon as the coast is clear – and one should not expose the nest so that magpies or crows will spot it more easily.

If you look for nests in the hedges at the beginning of April, you are most likely to find those of the song-thrush, which are among the earliest breeders. Their stout mud nests, covered with grass on the outside but quite bare inside, are easy to see. The four or five eggs that the hen will lay are pure turquoise, with just a few black spots at the larger end. Inevitably, many of these early clutches are lost, but the birds nest again quickly, and usually with better luck. They may go on to a second or even a third successful brood before summer is over.

Even easier to find, sometimes, are the nests of long-tailed tits. I have just been watching a pair hanging on to the struts of an old fence and tearing off tiny pieces of moss and cobweb off them. They build their domed nest from the inside, weaving the moss together using the cobwebs. They leave an entrance hole at the top, but it closes naturally and is hard to see. Here it would be a mistake to put one's fingers in to feel the eggs or to take them out for a look; one could hardly avoid doing damage. Later, when the young have flown, one sometimes finds an addled egg left behind – white with pink spots, and very small.

Long-tailed Tit

Warm weather in early April sets many other birds nesting. Starlings and house sparrows are going under the eaves of buildings with straw and feathers. The first female hedge sparrows are building their neat, mossy nests, sometimes with two males in attendance, both of them singing in the yellow forsythia.

A few early robins are carrying leaves about: they nest most often in holes in the hedgebanks but they will sometimes use holes in the ground. I remember once bending down in a birch wood to pick up something I had dropped, and finding myself looking into the beady black eyes and red face of a robin incubating in a hollow among the brown leaf litter.

Small birds hardly ever use their nests again, but the crow family – rooks, carrion crows and magpies – often go back to their substantial old nests, and are busy repairing them or beginning to lay eggs.

All these are resident British birds. It will be a little longer before any of the newly arrived summer visitors begin to think of nesting.

About five million willow warblers invade the British Isles each year and settle down as two-and-a-half million pairs. But this vast migration goes practically unnoticed.

The willow warbler is the commonest of all our summer visitors, yet it is almost unknown compared to the swallow or the nightingale.

Its song is its most distinctive characteristic. It is a trickling cadence, starting high and sharp, and falling to lower, sweeter notes. Willow warblers are close relatives of the chiffchaffs that started arriving in March, and are very similar to look at; they are small, olive-green birds, of a group called 'leaf warblers'. However, the chiffchaff's two clinking notes come generally from high treetops, whereas the willow warbler sings its more delicate song in smaller trees in birch woods and spinneys.

Willow warblers have spent the winter well to the south in Africa – nobody knows precisely where the British birds go, since Africa in December is packed with sojourning willow warblers from most of Europe and half of Asia. What we do know is that there have been some adverse weather conditions in recent years, either in the willow warblers' winter quarters or on their migration routes, because there has been a slight drop in the summer population here.

Another warbler has been following hard on the hind claws of the willow warblers: the blackcap. This species, by contrast, has been rather more numerous here in recent summers.

This is the time to get a good look at them, before the leaves grow dense. They dart rapidly from one tree to the next, with an outburst of song every time they pause. Occasionally you get an excellent view for a moment or two, and can see the silvery-grey body, the light-brown back, and the smart, black skull-cap.

After a few hesitant notes, each passage of song turns into a rich, passionate outpouring, one of the finest bird songs you can hear in Britain. Sometimes, when one is listening out for newly arrived blackcaps, one can momentarily be deceived by a robin. Robins often begin with a sudden, brilliant flow of notes, that might just be a blackcap – but almost at once they modulate into their unmistakable, plaintive diminuendo.

More difficult to distinguish, when they arrive towards the end of April, will be the garden warblers. If you see them, there is no problem: they have no black cap. In fact, these graceful brown warblers are best identified in that they have no distinguishing marks at all. As for their songs, the blackcap's is generally more varied, with the notes clearly spaced out, while the garden warbler's is more of a sustained warble. But even ornithologists with well-trained ears are sometimes uncertain what they are hearing.

More blackcaps from the Continent have been wintering in Britain recently. In the county bird reports, the lists of 'First Date of Arrival of Summer Migrants' no longer include the blackcap, because observers are no longer quite sure which are winter and which are summer visitors. However, if you hear a blackcap singing in April you can be pretty sure that it has just come back from the Mediterranean to breed here.

One or two golden orioles can be expected to arrive before the month is out, though they are very scarce spring visitors. They sing in the treetops of large, deciduous woods, and seem to haunt long lines of tall poplars in particular.

I saw one a few years ago in a wood on the Oxfordshire–Gloucestershire border, and I think my experience was typical. Late in the evening, I suddenly heard a ringing 'woodley-woo' call in the distance. I had heard the golden oriole's song in Spain and was almost sure that this was what it was. I went off in pursuit, but every time I heard the song again it was coming from a different side – now deeper in the wood, now far away across a field. The sun set, and I had not seen the bird. Next morning, I went out early and to my delight (and relief) heard the note again almost immediately. But at the first the same thing happened. The bird seemed to be returning quite often to a particular stretch of the wood where there were some ornamental conifers among the oak and hornbeam, so I took up a position where I had a good view of these trees. Then, at last, I saw it. It swept up to one of the treetops from below and perched on the crest. It was unmistakable – a large, alert bird, bright yellow with black wings. It swayed on the thin spray, then swooped down and away. I saw it once more when it returned to the same perch, but I never saw it flying through the trees. It was amazing that this brilliantly coloured bird could move about so invisibly. It was shy, devious and fast-flying. So your ear is what you need to find a golden oriole.

With all the excitement of birds arriving from the south, it is easy to forget that a large departure to the north has also been taking place. The redwings and fieldfares sometimes announce their intention to leave. In the early spring, both species gather in flocks in treetops on the edge of the fields, and warble in a rambling, jangly way.

Sometimes I have heard the last of them singing like that while the song of a chiffchaff comes distinctly across the field from another woodland edge – the voices of winter and summer mingling.

Cuckoo! You hear the call a long way off, and you head towards it, scanning the treetops.

But all too often it remains a 'wandering voice', falling silent, then mocking you again from as far away as ever. Yet sometimes you get an unexpected view of a cuckoo. The one I remember best was at Kyleakin, on the Isle of Skye.

I had come across on the five-minute ferry trip from Kyle of Lochalsh the evening before and, first thing the next morning, I went up the hill above the village. I could hear a cuckoo calling up there (it had woken me up), and as soon as I got to the top, I saw it sitting on a telephone wire – this was Skye, and there were no trees around.

It was putting on its usual performance as it called – drooping its wings, spreading its tail, lifting its head high on the 'cuck' and letting it fall on the 'oo'.

But what was remarkable was the echo. Opposite us, across the blue sea-channel, was a line of mountains – and every time the cuckoo called its cry came echoing back through the still air from the mainland of Scotland.

Cuckoos return to Britain from Africa in the second half of April, and are soon heard all over the country. If you see one flying, it can remind you of a hawk: it is blue-grey, like a male sparrow-hawk, and it has pointed wings and a long tail like a falcon.

But it is not hard to distinguish from the hawk: it has a very peculiar flight, unusually straight, and never bringing its wings above the horizontal. The male, in any case, commonly calls when it is flying; the female, which looks similar, has a loud bubbling call.

Few birds have an odder way of life. The males occupy song territories, and the females take up egg-laying territories, but they all seem to mate very promiscuously.

The females then begin their 'research' into the local meadow pipits, hedge sparrows, or reed warblers. Each female cuckoo concentrates its attention on one of those species – on the moors, for instance, you mainly find 'meadow pipit cuckoos' and in farmland 'hedge sparrow cuckoos'. Occasionally they may also turn their attention to other species, such as robins.

They watch the small birds building, and once a female starts laying, the cuckoo comes down in the afternoon, removes one of the other bird's eggs and lays one of her own in the nest. The cuckoo egg is bigger and may even be a different colour, but the pipit or warbler accepts it.

The cuckoo egg hatches slightly sooner than the other eggs in the nest, and the young cuckoo that emerges does not take long to heave out the other eggs or tiny nestlings. The deluded 'parents' then feed it until it is a brown avian monster, far larger than themselves. With its screaming cry, the cuckoo chick may even persuade other parent birds to join in the good work. Nor does it hesitate to peck its foster-parents if it is hungry or otherwise dissatisfied with them.

Its true mother, meanwhile, pays no more attention to it. She goes on prowling round the countryside, even destroying nests of her host species that already contain eggs or young, so that they will have to build another nest and lay again for her convenience.

The female cuckoo generally lays an egg every other day, probably producing about 12 in an average year. As the summer wears on, the male cuckoo's call deteriorates, and you hear curious 'cuck-cuckoo' sounds. All the cuckoos, young and old, are on their way to Africa by early August.

For years, controversy raged over whether female cuckoos laid direct into their victims' nests, or whether they laid the egg nearby, then picked it up with their beak and put it in.

In the years before the Second World War, a painstaking but irascible naturalist, Edgar Chance, proved that the female cuckoo always lays her egg directly into the nest, though sometimes she has problems with an awkwardly placed nest, and the egg falls to the ground. When that happens, she lets it lie.

Chance recorded his findings in a book called *The Truth About the Cuckoo*. It is one of the most entertaining bird books I know – not least because he deals with opponents of his arguments about as mercilessly as the young cuckoo deals with its fellow-nestlings.

Several birds have a loud, piping 'pee-pee-pee' call. The commonest is the nuthatch, and it is very vocal in the treetops just now, sometimes hanging upside-down as it shouts. You can hear a remarkably similar cry from a kestrel flying round a tall building that it is nesting on: I heard it over Trinity House by the Tower of London the other day. A slower, more mellow version comes from the lesser spotted woodpecker, high in the trees in spring.

However, one April day a few years ago, among some old oaks and sweet chestnuts in Windsor Great Park, I had a surprise. I heard just such a call, and lifted my field-glasses expecting to find another nuthatch in the tree ahead of me. But sitting across a low branch I found something quite different: a scaly brown bird, barred underneath, that was twisting its neck like a snake as it looked at me. It was a wryneck – that very well-named bird!

As I watched it, it turned and climbed up a vertical bit of the branch, then sat across the top of it, wriggling its neck once more. I had time to study the fine, nightjar-like pattern of its plumage before it flew off. I heard it calling in the distance and went in pursuit, but did not find it again.

Nevertheless, I had been very lucky to see it, because there is rarely more than one pair of wrynecks found breeding in England each year. Quite a few migrate up the coast, and some breed in Scotland occasionally. Besides these, a few more, like my bird, settle and call in English woods and parks. They fail to get mates and soon disappear.

Wrynecks are curious birds – members of the woodpecker family, but not very much like the other British woodpeckers. For one thing they are migrants, whereas the others do not go far from their native woods. Also, they do not drill their own holes to nest in, but use existing holes. They like open woods because they feed mainly on the ground, on ants. They have a very long, flickering tongue, five times the length of their beak, with which they plunder the anthills. April is the month to go and look for them. Their call is very like the nuthatch's, but a little louder and stronger. And if you only find an upside-down nuthatch – well, that will not be so bad either.

About 1,000 pairs of little ringed plovers come to nest in Britain every summer. Humans are their friends: they settle almost invariably in places we have made. The stony shores of gravel pits are their favourite nesting-sites, but they also breed on the dried sludge at sewage farms, and by reservoirs. Men working around them are also their friends, because they keep off daytime predators such as kestrels and sparrow-hawks.

They are small black, brown and white birds that with their broken head-and-breast markings are almost invisible against the stones. They are very like slightly larger ringed plovers that are common along our coasts, but a few points distinguish them clearly. They have a thin white line above the black band on their forehead, and their legs are flesh-coloured, not bright orange as are the larger birds.

Little Ringed Plover

Also, when they fly they show no white wing-bar, and their 'tee-oo' call puts the accent on the first syllable, while the ringed plover's 'too-lee' emphasizes the second. That last difference may sound a rather faint one, but it is amazing how clear it is once you hear them!

Little ringed plovers have only been here for just over 50 years – the first pair bred at Tring in 1938. On the Continent they nest mainly on pebbly river-banks; and recently they have expanded their conquests in Wales, reverting to similar sites.

On the stones, they run fast with twinkling feet, and in April they are busy there. The male makes scrapes among the stones, and the female will choose one of them to lay her eggs in. In their courting display, he sits in a scrape lifting his tail, then gets up; she passes under his tail and squats in the scrape herself. He approaches her with a kind of high quickstep and finally they mate. It is like a plovers' ballet.

The male also dances over his territory with a butterfly-like flight to warn off other males, singing a thin song. But after the four blotchy, stone-coloured eggs have been laid, the plovers fall silent and are harder to track down.

Both members of the pair incubate and feed the young, which start running about soon after they are hatched. The parents get noisier again when looking after the fledglings; they also put on dramatic displays to lure away intruders, dragging a wing piteously along the ground as if it were broken.

Gravel pits are important nowadays for other birds. More often than not the abandoned workings are left to themselves, and willows and reeds grow up around them. Local wildlife trusts have taken some over, and manage them as nature reserves.

The end of April brings a cheerful sound to many of them. It is the song of the sedge warblers in the reeds or, more often, in bramble bushes along the banks.

Sometimes the singer skulks unseen on the far side of the bush, sometimes it sings boldly from a thorny spray, and sometimes it even shoots straight up into the air as it sings, and comes dropping down again, with its wings and tail spread.

If you get a good view, you cannot mistake it. It is a small bird with a creamy-yellow eyestripe, a streaky brown back and a gingery rump that is very noticeable when it flies away from you.

As for the song, there is nothing quite like it. It begins with a monotonous chinking, and sometimes does not get any further than that. But usually the chinking gives way to an amazing hodge-podge of lively sounds – trills and whistles, and creaking notes and imitations of other birds, even of the coot's piercing cry and the clattering alarm call of the blackbird.

These songsters are all male birds, singing to attract a mate. Their voices often ring out wonderfully in the night in the last days of April. Females may be passing overhead in the dark – and they may be tempted down to take a look at the singer when morning comes.

The only bird you can confuse with the sedge warbler is the reed warbler, which clambers up and down the reeds in the same way. But it is a plain brown bird, and its song is like those mechanical opening notes of the sedge warbler's song, without any subsequent take-off into wild harmonies. Only dull, unenterprising sedge warblers sound like reed warblers.

The reed warbler's nest is more attractive, however. It is a deep cup attached to three or four reed stalks and hanging down between them. The sedge warbler has a simple, shallower nest in a bush or, sometimes nowadays, in a tangle of oilseed rape in a field near water.

Nightingales are rarer than they used to be: as Richard Mabey says in his book, *Whistling in the Dark,* about the great nocturnal songster, 'the national population has plummeted from tens of thousands of pairs in the 1950s to probably no more than 2,000 pairs in the 1990s.'

Yet in the last two weeks of April, there are still some arriving from Africa every year. In Kent, you may see a very russety bird flit low, like a robin, across the road in front of you, and then hear a burst of the amazing song from the spinney it flew into. In Suffolk, on the common above Minsmere, you may hear four or five all singing together from the depths of the blackthorn – and then see yet another singing and swaying on the top of a gorse bush.

Nightingales sing all day, as well as for much of the night. The night song will be heard mainly at the end of April when the males are trying to attract a mate.

It has two supreme phrases: the deep, throbbing 'jug-jug-jug-jug-jug' and the ravishing crescendo, louder and fuller with every note, 'piu-piu-piu-piu-piu'.

In between, there is a turbulent medley of croaks, trills and sweet liquid notes that is suddenly left behind as the bird's voice modulates into one of the classic passages. In the silence of the night it can be heard half a mile away.

Nightingales are members of the thrush family, like robins, and they have some of the robin's ways. Their plumage is simpler – russet brown above, chestnut at the base of the tail, paler beneath – but they sit on a low twig and study the ground below with their head cocked, just like a robin. Then they drop down to the ground to feed, on ants, spiders and beetles.

Few people have seen them doing this, since much of their life goes on deep among the undergrowth. Their nests, too, are well hidden in the bottom of bushes – bulky nests, usually with a foundation of oak leaves, where, eventually, there will be four or five olive-brown or olive-green eggs.

Tennyson, in one of his poems, says 'the music of the moon/Sleeps in the plain eggs of the nightingale'. The female nightingale incubates the eggs alone, while the male goes on singing. But once the eggs have hatched he helps her feed the nestlings, and the song is not heard much more.

Both the parents feed the young birds in the nest, and when the young fly, they often break up into two groups, one of them in the care of the male and the other in the care of the female. These fledglings are like young robins, very mottled and spotty, except that like their parents they have chestnut tails. Song is over by this stage, usually some time in June, but the adult nightingales are still very noisy, warning their offspring of any danger with harsh churring notes. However, as the early nineteenth-century poet John Clare said in *The Nightingale's Nest*, which gives a very accurate account of nightingale behaviour, 'the old prickly thorn bush guards them well'.

In Britain, nightingales usually have only one brood. Like the cuckoo, they are on the move by July. By the end of August they have crossed the Sahara desert and are singing again on the borders of the African rain forests.

In eastern Europe, a closely related species called the thrush-nightingale sings a similar song in town parks, and schoolchildren and students are distracted by the loud music as they prepare for their summer examinations.

However, in Britain, reports of city nightingales shattering the silence in the early hours of the morning are, I am sorry to say, usually wrong. While you may hear birds singing in the night in city centres, particularly where the lamps are bright, they are almost invariably robins or wrens, or song-thrushes anticipating the dawn.

Tree pipits are also back in Britain. They haunt the edges

Nightingale

of woods, where they fly up from a branch, then drop down singing on fluttering wings as though they were living parachutes. Whitethroats in the hedges and sedge warblers along ditchsides also throw themselves into the sky, then come down singing excitedly.

All of them are male birds who are trying to attract mates, and at the same time warn off other males.

But the nightingale has no need of such antics. It can sit in the darkness of a bush, or the blackness of the night, and let its song do all the work that the spring requires.

MAY

A flaming spirit is back in the woods of the west of England in May: it is called the common redstart. You will find it especially in airy woods and parkland, because it flies about a lot and needs plenty of space. It has a bright red tail, and as it flies it seems like a swooping light in the shadows beneath the trees. When it perches, its tail constantly quivers and trembles.

Altogether it is a beautiful bird. It is the size of a large robin, and the male has a red breast, a black face-mask topped with white and a pearl-grey back. The female is browner but also has the restless orange-red tail.

The species is not as widespread as it used to be. Its numbers appear to have suffered from drought in the southern Sahara, where it winters. But especially in the west of England, there are many redstarts singing and calling in the oak woods now. The song is short and rather clockwork-like, somehow suitable for such a brisk bird. You are more likely to detect it by its frequent calls, a sharp note followed by angry ticking.

It nests in holes in old trees, and this is when its colours are employed to greatest effect. The male courts the female by showing nest-holes to her: he peers out of the entrance, displaying the white band on his forehead, or else goes into the hole, pausing to vibrate his red tail behind him. At other times he will swoop conspicuously down to the hole from a nearby branch.

His flashing colours are also seen as he flies up to the female in courtship, or when he chases other males away, twisting and turning through the trees. Few birds animate the woodland so vigorously.

The other late summer visitors have also returned. Another bird that lives in the shade beneath the trees is the spotted flycatcher. But this is a sober-plumaged bird, inconspicuous until it darts out after an insect. Then you realize it has been sitting all the time on a low bough of the yew tree.

Looked at closely, you see that it actually has rather fine, streaky-brown plumage, with silvery-grey underparts, and also an interesting, hunched, alert look about it. Most often it flies up to take an insect with a snap of its beak, then returns to its lookout post. But if a fly dodges it, it will pursue it determinedly, wheeling and twisting as if on hairpin bends.

It likes to nest in wistaria on the side of a house, and when its young fledge, the garden is suddenly full of activity, as well as a great deal of noise from the anxious parents. Churchyards are a favourite haunt, and I have sometimes seen a whole family of them all sitting on different tombstones, the parents hunting and the young crying out to be fed.

Also just arriving are the lesser whitethroats. This is a mysterious bird, not often observed though constantly heard. Its main song is generally described as a loud rattle, although I think it is really more like a rapid peal on a cracked and tuneless bell. It is quite common and can be heard a long way away.

You will generally find that the singer is in the heart of a tall hedge or small hawthorn tree, impossible to see except as a shape glimpsed among the leaves and twigs. You also discover that it has another completely contrasting song – a whispered little prelude of sweet and harsh notes before it bursts out with the full peal.

Just occasionally the singer will come out of the bush and give you a good view of it. It has a gleaming white throat, but is greyer than the common whitethroat and also has a dark patch over each ear.

When the common whitethroat was seriously down in numbers about 20 years ago after the southern Saharan drought, the lesser whitethroat was probably, for a time, the more abundant species, though the common whitethroat has now overtaken it again. The lesser whitethroat is unusual among summer visitors because it flies south-east, not south, in autumn, and winters in Egypt and the eastern Mediterranean.

Blood-curdling screams in the skies are another sound that tells you some summer birds are back. You hear them coming rapidly towards you, then a party of swifts explodes into sight and whirls over the roofs. Their long, narrow wings flicker into the distance and they vanish. But a few minutes later they are rushing past again. Forget the music of the countryside: this urban din is the surest sign that we are on the verge of summer.

White wings are flickering over estuaries in many parts of Britain early in May, as little terns arrive from Africa. They are the smallest British terns and are easily identified by their white forehead under the black cap, and their yellow beak with a black tip. They have a more butterfly-like flight than the other terns, and hover for longer over the water before diving in with a splash to pick up a fish. You often hear them before you see them, chattering shrilly above the water; then the sun flashes on them as they flit past, wheel round, and start hovering.

They nest on the coast, on sand and shingle beaches, but they like to work their way up the shallow water of the estuaries when out fishing. On the beaches they are easily disturbed by bathers, and some of their nesting-sites are now protected by fences. In a big colony in County Wicklow in Ireland, individual wire fences have been constructed round the nests in recent years, to keep off rats and foxes – but in 1990 the site wardens were defeated by a kestrel who swooped down on some of the chicks. There are not more than about 2,500 pairs nesting in this country, but there is a fair chance of seeing one or two almost anywhere along the shore at this time.

An even more conspicuous estuary bird just now is the shelduck, with its white body, green head, and chestnut breast-band. At present, the drakes are spending a lot of time guarding their mates while they dabble for food at the sea's edge or in the pools among the sand. The duck lays up to ten large, creamy-coloured eggs, and she needs a great deal of food to be able to do this. So the males stand by, keeping off predators and other drakes. They menace their rivals with lowered heads and necks, and will chase away even other species of duck, like shovelers. They are big, powerful birds, almost the size of a goose, and a shoveler quickly flees.

Shelduck make their nests, which are lined with the female's down, in rabbit holes and in hollow trees. Their numbers have been increasing lately, and more and more are going some way inland to nest.

There is plenty of other bird life on the estuary. Over the salt marshes behind the seawall, skylarks are singing. A redshank hurtles by with loud, musical cries; it skims over the sea-wall and lands by a pool, pointing its white-barred wings at the sky for a moment before folding them. It will be nesting in the fields just inland. Black-and-white oyster-catchers are piping in the distance – they could be nesting either in the fields or among the pebbles. A few dunlin running along the sand are probably just stopping off to feed on their way to Scotland. A swallow from a coastal farm is swooping down and dipping into the sea, briefly bathing, not far from where the terns are still fishing.

There is a yelp from the redshank and off it dashes again. Simultaneously the other birds on the shore take wing. They have all seen a sparrow-hawk that now swerves away back inland, hoping to achieve more surprise next time it targets a wader. Birds, like humans, find plenty to interest them where the sea meets the land.

The lowlands of Scotland turn red in mid-May. I am not talking of political passions, but of the red campion lining the roadside and the woodland edges. It is a good moment to be there – especially to make your way along a lowland glen in hills such as the Lammermuirs or the Pentlands.

On grassy slopes going up from the burn, a clamour breaks out: a carrion crow has settled on the hillside, and a curlew is making loud, plaintive calls, swooping down on it. The crow cringes as the big mottled wings beat above it, passing within inches of its head. The curlews have begun to incubate among the scraggy gorse and are not giving the crow a meal of new-laid eggs.

As you climb higher, there is more and more yellow gorse in flower and wafts of its scent, something like burnt toffee, come rolling down. On the tufty grass between the gorse bushes, a flock of rooks and jackdaws is feeding noisily.

Now, down in the valley below, a curlew is beginning to trill – faster and faster, more and more ecstatic. It sweeps past you, wings trembling, beak open like curved tongs.

Curlew

What is that bright object, visible down there in the field beyond the burn? It is an oyster-catcher sitting on its nest, unable to conceal its black and white feathers and long red beak. With the help of its mate it will defend the eggs as fiercely as the curlews.

The hills are getting higher, but now the road turns down and meets the burn once more. A small, moth-like shape skims away across the water with a scolding note, but when it settles, you can see it is a brown bird, with a white breast edged at the bottom with orange. It is a dipper, the quintessential bird of rocky streams.

It is feeding down there on the stream bed. Suddenly, it emerges and whirrs away once more. However, you know you will see it again. Its territory will come to an end where the next dipper's begins.

Common sandpipers have just arrived back, and you are approaching a perfect site for them. The banks of the burn open out, and it winds its way through a broad stretch of

Dipper

pebbles. A light brown bird with a white wing-bar, its flickering wing beats and tittering call are unmistakable.

The path is winding up the slope again now and heather is taking over. Suddenly the whole hillside opposite bursts into sound. Barking noises, gobbling noises, then a loud clear call: 'Go-back, go-back'. It is the red grouse courting and quarrelling. But where are they? At last there is a movement – a black shape is on the wing, and it lands. You see the stocky outline of the grouse – and there just beyond it is another, which your bird has come to chase. It is a wonderful place up there, with the grouse cackling, the skylarks and meadow pipits singing – and now another curlew hurling itself at a crow, its ringing cries drowning everything.

It sounds like chaos on the cliff face. Hundreds of guillemots are standing on the ledges shoulder to shoulder, and on every jutting bit of rock a kittiwake is sitting on its nest of green seaweed. The harsh, rolling cries of the guillemots blend into a roar through which you can just hear the kittiwakes repeating their name – 'kittiwek, kittiwek'.

But this is not chaos at all. Many of these birds have come back to exactly the same spot on the cliff where they nested last year, and they know exactly where they are now.

The guillemots are just starting to lay, and all their eggs will be slightly different – from blue to white, with rich mottling – so that they will always recognize their own. (It helps that each pair has only one egg.) And before the chick is completely out of the egg, it will be making its own personal call and learning to recognize its parents' voices.

I have just been watching the guillemot spectacle at St Abb's Head, on the Scottish coast east of Dunbar. There are several cliffs and rock stacks here without a vacant flat spot on them, and from some points you can watch the birds from very close.

The air around is full of whizzing and floating forms. Guillemots coming back to the cliff rocket through the air on tiny wings, and brake before they land by aiming just below the ledge, then swooping up against the pull of gravity.

The snow-white kittiwakes drift between the cliffs, an occasional stiff-winged fulmar glides among them, and out at sea gannets beat majestically by. The gannets' base is the Bass Rock, 20 miles up the coast on the Firth of Forth.

As you lie among the pink thrift, scrutinizing the cliff face opposite, you begin to sort out what is happening. The guillemots stand upright, or lean forwards against a bit of sloping rock. They are black above, shining white beneath. Among them are a few of the 'brindled' variety, with white spectacles round their eyes. The guillemots are so close to each other that they quarrel all the time, especially when one of the pair comes to relieve the other – or to practise a little courtship, when they rub their sharp black bills together.

Here and there among the guillemots stands a pair of razorbills. They are more densely black on the back than the guillemots, and can sometimes be picked out by that, but the main difference is that they have a thicker bill, curved at the tip, with a distinct vertical line on it. They prefer ledges with some sort of overhanging roof, and their eggs are rounder than the guillemots'. The pronounced pear shape of the guillemots' eggs is thought to be a safety device, since it means they roll round in a circle and not off the edge into the sea.

At present, there are usually two kittiwakes on each nest, billing like the guillemots and occasionally mating. This is when you hear the 'kittiwek' call.

It is a species that has become far more common in this century than it was in the last, when large numbers were killed and their white wing feathers used to adorn hats. They have now colonized other nest-sites beside cliff faces, and not far away at Dunbar you can get very close to them on the castle ruins.

The other main species nesting at St Abb's is the shag – a big black bird with a wonderful, glossy-green sheen which has its nest lower down in cave-like hollows. On the grassy turf at the top of the cliffs, herring gulls stalk about. Whenever they see a chance, they steal an egg from one of the cliff-nesters, but the massed infantry of the guillemots is usually too much for them.

The next stage will be the hatching of the guillemot chicks. They are very vulnerable on the open ledges, and they leave their birthplace long before their feathers are fully grown.

When the moment has come for them to jump, their parents bustle encouragingly about them, and suddenly they make a wild, fluttering descent on stubs of wings down to the sea. Their parents go on feeding them on the water for a while, and slowly the family moves further out. Long before summer is over, the cliffs will be silent again.

About the last small birds to start nesting in this country are the goldfinches. This is because they like to feed their young on mashed-up thistle seeds, and the thistles will not be scattering their down much before the beginning of June.

In mid-May, the goldfinches are flying about in pairs, looking for nest sites. They are always a brilliant sight. As they lilt and dip through the air, their gold-barred wings flash in the sun. The very moment they settle, they seem poised to go again, but for an instant you may get a clear view of their red, white and black heads, and if one turns to face you, you can see the buff patches on either side of the white chest.

The birds' courtship display – also to be seen now – makes full use of their colours. They crouch with wings spread to reveal all their gold feathers, and the red 'blaze' on their forehead is puffed up. In this posture, they swing from side to side.

There is a courtship flight – the 'moth' flight – in which the pair fly around with shallow wing beats. The males also perform a 'butterfly' routine, in which they fly around singing, with slow, deep wing beats, their feathers all fluffed out.

Goldfinches are not very territorial. They defend a small area around the apple or cherry tree where they will make their nest, but it has been calculated that you could get 30 pairs of goldfinches into the average chaffinch territory. Not that you are likely to find quite so many pairs nesting side by side in reality.

The neat but deep nest of moss and roots and lichen, bound together with spiders' webs and well-lined with down and hair, is usually built at the end of a swaying branch. There are four to six red-speckled eggs, and the female goldfinch sits on them day and night for about 12 days. She occasionally comes off for a little exercise, and to bathe, but she is generally fed on the nest by the male, and gets very excited, shivering her wings and begging, when he arrives with food.

The incubation period is the only time of year when these lively, restless birds seem to relax. For long periods, the male will sit on a conspicuous twig high in a lime or ash tree, and sing continuously. This is a characteristic sight of early June. His song is not exactly beautiful, but it is utterly delightful.

All year round, goldfinches utter a stream of tinkling, bell-like notes as they fly. The song is a richer version of these, with plummy notes among the light ripples.

After that, it is hard work again for both sexes. They share the task of feeding the young, usually mixing in a few insects with the seeds. The fledglings leave the nest after a fortnight. They have the gold-striped wings of their parents but their heads and bodies are grey, and they are called 'grey pates'.

A second, even a third brood, follows. By August the countryside will be full of goldfinch families, flocking not only to the thistle tops but coming down to our lawns and roadside verges to pluck at the dandelion clocks and the ragwort seeds.

It used to be thought that goldfinches were resident birds, but it is now known that most of them go south in autumn. A few will linger in Britain, brightening the winter days, but by January the rest will be enjoying the luxurious seed-fare of the Mediterranean countries.

Many people have been anxiously scanning the skies above their house at the end of May in recent years. They have been hoping to see their house martins wheeling and darting about up there, making their clicking cries, before coming down to build their mud nests under the eaves again.

For some years now, fewer house martins have returned here for the summer. No one has established with any certainty the cause of the drop in numbers, though it is probably due to adverse weather somewhere on their long migration route up from southern Africa – perhaps in the Sahara desert.

In what used to be a normal year, most house martins would have been building, and some of them laying, by now.

House martins are birds of the middle air, feeding entirely on flying insects. They share the sky with the swifts, who fly higher, and in rural areas with the swallows, who tend to fly lower. Sometimes, over lakes in midsummer, you can see all three layers of birds together.

The house martins even gather their nest-linings – scraps of straw, and feathers – on the wing. But they are earthbound when they collect their main building material – mud.

They settle by puddles or at the edge of rivers to pick it up, and are often quite tame at such times. At least a wet summer ensures that those individuals who have made the journey back will be able to build their nests easily.

Meanwhile those resident birds who began nesting last month are seeing their young come out into the world. The most noticeable are the young blackbirds, all brown like their mothers. When they leave the nest, they break up into two groups, each of two or three birds.

One group is looked after by the female, the other by the male. They lurk under hedges and bushes making sharp

Song-thrush

cries for the first week or so, then start hopping out to meet their parent when it brings food. When the female starts a second brood, the male takes over all of the first brood.

Young song-thrushes behave in much the same way, though the family does not split up. Throughout this period, both thrushes and blackbirds go on singing in the morning and evening to warn intruders of their territories. Mistle-thrushes also sing on into the long days of summer.

Counts of song-thrushes suggest that there has been a fall in numbers, but you cannot go far in country or suburb just now without hearing one. Sometimes you come across a song-battle; two male song-thrushes facing each other in a bush, singing for all they are worth, then flying at each other, fighting and singing again until one finally retreats – to an outburst of wild notes from the victor.

JUNE

An excited squeaky buzz is coming from the depths of the bushes. You may have heard it sometimes in April, when it was the call of the female robin being fed by her mate during courtship. Now it is the call of the fledgling robins as they, in turn, are being fed. Soon the woods and gardens will be full of the sound.

Like many young birds, the robins look different from their parents: they will not acquire the red breast till the autumn moult, and at present are dappled brown above and spotty beneath. When their mother begins a second brood, they will remain in the charge of their father for a few days. After that they will settle down to an idle summer, with plenty of caterpillars to feed on.

Many such unfamiliar sounds will be heard in the countryside in June. Young blackbirds have a distinctive squeak, and there will be millions of those about: there are thought to be about seven million pairs of blackbirds breeding in the British Isles every summer. The fledglings are also easily picked out: they have a more rufous tint than the dark-brown females and, like the young robins, are spotty below.

Greenfinches have a wheezing note, like a long sucking kiss; their young, which are grey rather than green, have even more long-drawn-out, slurping calls, which they repeat interminably in the heart of a flowering elder or a rhododendron on a sunny afternoon. Young brown starlings bully their parents noisily on the lawn or in the trees, flying furiously after them when they try to escape.

Jacques

Blue Tit

Young titmice will soon be out and about, calling to their parents; sometimes there are 10 or 12 from a single nest. The newly fledged blue tits lack the blue cap of their parents but are more yellow all over; young coal tits are also yellow beneath, where their parents are greyish-white.

All these small songbirds are featherless and blind when they hatch out; they stay in the nest for a fortnight or so while they grow their feathers and are then fed for a few more weeks after they have flown.

Young skylarks have a slightly different life. The nest is on the ground, among long grass or growing corn, and they are very vulnerable there. So, although their flight feathers take the usual fortnight to grow, they leave the nest after about eight days, and hide in the foliage around them until they can fly.

Some larger birds, notably the waders, have nidifugous young – that is to say, birds which leave the nest as soon as they have struggled out of the eggshell. Young lapwings trot away into the undergrowth; their parents resolutely chase off predators. In fact, meadow pipits sometimes nest in lapwings' territories, because the carrion or hooded crows are driven away.

All this care for the young comes from the fact that nature selects birds who bring up most offspring. Among the small birds, the young usually hatch out all together and grow up at the same speed. But with some larger birds, such as tawny owls, who may find it hard to get enough food, the young hatch out at intervals, and the earlier ones are the stronger.

In a good year for food, all the owl nestlings will get enough to eat; but in a bad year, the stronger will take most of it, and the weaker will die. In either event, the parent owls will have brought up the maximum possible number under the circumstances. Birds may show devotion to their young – but nature itself is not loving.

Looking out over a lake in early June, you may think there is something wrong with your eyes. A great crested grebe swimming some way from the shore has two heads – or did, a moment ago.

It is not a hallucination. For a moment it did have two heads – and one belonged to a young grebe riding on its back, hidden beneath the wings until it put its head up and had a look round.

Great crested grebes are remarkable birds. They are very handsome, in a Satanic way; they have a gaudy chestnut ruff and a fierce, dagger-like beak, and when they face you, their dark ear-tufts, meeting in front above the beak, look like a pair of sinister eyebrows. Then they have this startling habit of taking their small young around with them.

When the adult dives, the tiny, striped chicks usually float off its back, although sometimes they go under and come up again still clinging on. They make their way across the water to their other parent and clamber up there.

Not all of this summer's young grebes are out of the egg yet. Further along the lake there is a solitary great crested grebe, staring at you suspiciously as it slowly patrols a patch of thin reeds. Somewhere in there its mate is sitting on a floating nest.

A pair of tufted ducks is also swimming idly in front of the reed-bed. The drake is black with a white patch on the flank, the female dark brown, and both have bright yellow eyes with which they too are watching you.

Tufted ducks are late nesters, and this pair is still waiting to build a nest somewhere on the lake shore. Eventually the duck will lay between 8 and 18 white eggs – and if, as sometimes happens, another one uses the same nest, they will end up with an enormous pile of eggs.

Under some overhanging willow boughs there is more activity. A coot has just dived, and around the ripples are some curious birds, dark above, silvery-grey beneath, and revealing a bright red mouth as they make piteous, piping notes. They are the coot's family, already growing up, but still begging.

When the parent surfaces, the first thing it does is to swim hard at one of them and try to peck it. Coots are irascible birds and get as angry with their young as with other coots that try to invade their territory. However, next time it dives it comes up with some water weed and gives it to one of the pleading offspring.

There are coots further along – a younger family this time. The tiny birds that are fizzing about on the water are at this stage totally different from their parents. They look like coloured toys: orange round the neck, yellow on the back. They were out on the water almost as soon as they hatched, but they will go back to the nest, or rest on other reed platforms specially built for them, until they are a little larger.

Yet another family is close inshore round the headland: two Canada geese, with five goslings. The adult Canada geese are used to being fed by passers-by, so they do not move off as you approach them – but their instinct is nevertheless to threaten you. They crinkle their black and white necks, then immediately straighten them, so that their heads bob up and down; and as you get to the waters' edge, they start hissing at you.

The goslings are still small, and covered with fine golden down. As the party swims off, the young birds are shepherded by their parents, one slightly in front on one side, one at the back on the other.

The waterfowl are not the only lake-users. Sedge warblers are singing a jerky song in the osiers; a reed warbler is producing an even more scrappy song in the reed-bed, as it hangs on to a stem with one foot above the other. And over the water the swifts are hurtling. They rocket up into the air, and shoot far away over the reeds; a moment later you can hear the rush of their wings above your head as they return. They are just about to nest and are building up their strength with a feast of aquatic flies before the rigours of family life begin.

Swallows go wherever there are flying insects. They patrol up and down the rivers; they swoop in front of golfers who have disturbed the flies in the grass. They are instantly recognizable, with their steely blue backs and the 3in-long streamers either side of their tails, and you can often hear the snap of their beaks as they pick up an insect.

Most are nesting in early June, with eggs or young in the little mud cups that they have built on the rafters in dark barns and garages. They sweep through the door or window with amazing precision.

The pair defend their nest site against other swallows, and they will sometimes even chase bats away. After the first brood is on the wing, they will normally have a second and sometimes a third. So by the autumn, the fields around the farms are full of swallows, among whom the young can be distinguished because their streamers have not yet grown. By September, most are off to southern Africa; but a few late breeders stay around until October.

The two other members of the swallow family that breed in Britain are the house martin and the sand martin. House martins are black above, with a slight blue gloss, and white beneath, with white feathers on their legs. In the air they show a conspicuous white rump, and their chattering calls always remind me of the clicker that lantern-slide lecturers used to use when they wanted the picture changed.

After the young birds have flown, they still come back to the nest to roost for a time. The young of the first brood have also been recorded as helping their parents to feed the nestlings of the second annual family – an unusual form of co-operation among birds.

The smallest and least familiar of our swallows is the sand martin. It, too, comes up from central Africa, and its numbers were badly hit by the drought on the southern edge of the Sahara about 20 years ago. Also, it breeds mainly in holes in sandbanks and quarries, and that kind of nesting-site has become harder to find in recent years.

The nest-hole is the centre of their lives. They dig it out for themselves and usually come back to it in subsequent years. Unmated males sit in the entrance to attract a female. Paired birds will also sit there, ruffling up their head and neck feathers, to keep others out. When the young grow bigger they come to the entrance to watch out for their parents returning with food. At this time the young birds also learn to recognize their parents' individual calls: once they leave the nest, it would be easy to lose them among the sand martins that are constantly flying to and fro in front of the quarry face.

All the swallow family like sunbathing – swallows

sometimes lie on a roof, sand martins gather on the ground in the lee of a wall or cliff face. They turn their flanks to the sun and lift their wings to let the heat get to their bodies. Then they are off again on the endless quest for flying insects. They are birds of the sun and air, a tribe like no other.

Young blue tits have been popping out of holes everywhere – holes in trees, lamp-posts, old kettles and petrol-cans, flower-pots and nest-boxes in people's gardens. Sometimes as many as ten come flitting out one after the other into the wide world. They take refuge straight away in the depths of the dark-green June foliage, where they are easy to hear, but not easy to see. They keep up a perpetual hissing murmur, while their parents feed them indefatigably on caterpillars that they have picked up from the leaves of the oak and hazel trees.

The adults usually feed the young on large caterpillars, which they bring one at a time. Some caterpillars could inflict a nasty bite on the young birds' cheeks, so the parents kill them by knocking their heads sharply on a branch – and it would be hard to do that with more than one caterpillar in the beak. But if they are going to carry only one caterpillar, then it might as well be a large one. The parents themselves eat any small ones they encounter.

It has been estimated that in a normal June there may be up to 100,000 moth caterpillars gathered on a single oak tree. The breeding season of the tits has evolved to ensure that the young birds are being fed at this time of plenty.

If you do see the young birds, they are unmistakable. They look duller than the bright-blue adults, but have conspicuous yellow cheeks, whereas their parents' cheeks are white. They have gone through various hazards before getting out of the nest.

Blue tits have two surprising predators at this time – weasels and great spotted woodpeckers. Weasels are good tree-climbers, and often get into a blue tit's nest-hole and devastate the brood. Researchers into tit ecology in Wytham Wood, near Oxford, where there are large numbers of nest-boxes on the tree trunks, have sometimes climbed their aluminium ladders and opened the lid of a box only to have a weasel leap out at them.

Great spotted woodpeckers are too large to get into the holes – but they bore a hole of their own in the trunk, or in the wall of a nest-box, and get at the young that way.

The new broods will be left to their own devices about a fortnight after they leave the nest. Then they will have to come out of the leaves, and show themselves more. They will

Great Spotted Woodpecker

be mingling with young great tits, which also look rather drained of colour compared with the adults – apart, again from their characteristic yellow cheeks.

Young coal tits, too, feed in the oaks and birches, although they are commoner in conifer woods. They are the most distinctive fledglings of all these three species, as they have not only yellow cheeks, but also a marked yellow tinge to their wings.

The different species all feed together, but they remain rivals. Great tits will snatch food from blue tits, and both blue and great tits rob the even smaller coal tit. The coal tit's size gives it a further disadvantage: it loses heat more easily, and needs to spend longer each day looking for food. It is a deft little bird, though, as people who have seen it at their bird tables will know; rather than confront the larger birds, it will fly in swiftly to pick up morsels they have dropped.

Food may be plentiful now, but mortality hits the tits as the year goes on Usually, by the time spring comes, there are no more blue or great or coal tits around than there were the spring before. That means that from all these noisy families in the trees, perhaps only one adult and one fledgling will survive.

Cats, magpies and sparrow-hawks are all on the prowl. But for the moment, at any rate, in the long, warm summer days, the living is easy for the tits.

Pipits belong to the same group of birds as the larks. They are birds that evolved on the savannah grasslands of Africa but, as the forests of the north have disappeared, they have conquered most of the open spaces of the world.

The commonest pipit in this country, the meadow pipit, is found in almost any wild place where there is long, thick grass to nest in. But it is most abundant on the moors. It is a small, streaky brown bird, hard to see on the ground, but very conspicuous when the males are performing song-flights over their territories. They mount jerkily into the air with a lisping call, then parachute down with more musical notes, their wings and long tail lifted so that they look like a shuttlecock. There are almost two million pairs of them nesting in Britain, and the moors are alive with them in May.

They sometimes nest in a lapwing's territory, taking advantage of the larger bird's readiness to drive off crows; but the predator they suffer from most is the cuckoo. It is always easy to see a cuckoo on the moors because the only place it can sit is on the fences.

Each cuckoo generally preys on only one species of small bird, and these moorland cuckoos lay spotty brown eggs resembling the meadow pipit's. They lay one in every pipit's nest they can find, and the foster-parents do not detect the fraud, even though the cuckoo's egg is bigger. The young cuckoo, when it hatches, eventually throws out all the other eggs or nestlings.

Tree pipits are much more rarely parasitized by cuckoos. This seems to be because their eggs are more varied in their colouring and spottiness than the meadow pipit's. As a cuckoo cannot adapt each of its eggs to a particular nest, its alien offerings are more likely to be detected. No doubt the tree pipit has evolved this trait as a defence against cuckoos.

The third regular pipit in Britain is the rock pipit, which is a resident, is larger than the other two, and haunts rocky cliffs. In St Malo recently I watched some surprisingly domesticated individuals that regarded the town ramparts as cliffs, and fed at the top in the municipal gardens.

Pipits were once known as 'titlarks' – little larks. They may not sing like big larks, but I find them just as delightful to see.

Birds may be the winged creation for some, but their feet can be even more important. Two British birds that are always on their toes, so to speak, are the moorhen and the coot. They are both members of the rail family, which also includes the water-rail and the corncrake. All of them are short-winged and sturdy-footed, which enables them to move swiftly through dense vegetation.

Both moorhen and coot are water birds, but the moorhen is much less dependent on water. It has long toes with broad soles, so it can walk on thin mud or across lily leaves, without sinking; but it also spends a good deal of time feeding out in the fields. A flock of moorhens all scurrying back to the water's edge in alarm is a comic sight. They cock their tails, and the two white patches underneath, one on either side, look like flashing tail-lights.

Coots are more thoroughly adapted to water. They have lobed toes, like small paddles, and they use them to swim under water. They feed mainly on pond weed: they bring it up from the bottom and eat it when they get to the surface. While they are feeding in algae-covered water, their black bodies often get draped in a green coat.

Both coot and moorhen have a struggle to get up from the water, pattering frantically over it for a long way before they are airborne. However, both species fly quite well when they get going, and many coots from northern Europe travel to Britain and further south in the winter.

In June they can be found at all stages of the breeding cycle. They build substantial nests of reeds, either in reed-beds or out in shallow water. If the water rises, they will build them up still higher, until some coots' nests, especially, look like small towers. Often, too, the nests have a broad ramp of vegetation built on to one side so that the bird coming in to incubate can scramble up more easily.

Both species lay around six to ten blotchy brown eggs, but

occasionally you find twice that number in a nest. This is because these rails have a cuckoo-like streak in them. A female will lay a complete clutch of eggs in another female's nest, then go on to lay a clutch in her own – and if she is lucky will have double the offspring without any more work than usual.

Moorhen

Coots and moorhens are prolific, often having two large families a year. Some begin nesting early in spring, so by the end of June there are young birds out on the water of various ages. The chicks leave the nest as soon as they are hatched and follow their parents briskly through the dank vegetation.

Out on the water the chicks of the two species are easily distinguished. Both are tiny, blackish-brown balls, but the baby coots have orange-red heads and a trace of yellow on their backs. This is odd, because in the adults it is the moorhen that has a red shield above its beak, while the coot's shield is white.

As they grow older, the young moorhens grow more like their parents, but the young coots go through an intermediate stage when they have a dark body but a silvery throat and breast. These coot fledglings have puzzled many a bird-watcher.

Young coots and moorhens go on piping and squealing for food for many weeks. The adults are also still fighting loudly with each other, just as they did in the spring. So if there are coots and moorhens on a lake just now – and there usually are, because they are common birds – it will be a very noisy and animated scene, framed in the tranquil reeds and their reflections.

JULY

Herring gulls are the big gulls of the seaside – the ones you most commonly see following a boat, a flock of them usually, gliding effortlessly on the up-currents of air at the stern, occasionally diving down in a squalling mob to pick up a titbit from the water, then catching up with the boat again with a few powerful wing beats.

They can be distinguished by their cold yellow eyes, the yellow beak with a blood-red spot on it, and their pink legs. The smaller gull that is often found with them is the black-headed gull, easily picked out in summer by its chocolate-coloured hood.

Even people who would not recognize the herring gull often know its call: that loud, yelping laugh that rings out over the rooftops of seaside towns, sometimes from a bird on the wing, often from one sitting on a chimney-pot. In fact, you can distinguish between the different kinds of gull just by listening to their calls.

A small firm called Waxwing Associates has brought out an audio-cassette of seabird cries, in its excellent series *Teach Yourself Bird Sounds*. I believe the best way to learn bird songs and calls is to follow up every sound for oneself, get a view of the calling bird and identify it, and then commit the sound firmly to memory. But these cassettes are very good. Their information is accurate and they offer clear recordings of most of the calls of the different species, often putting them side by side for comparison.

For example, two close relatives of the herring gull, the great and the lesser black-backed gulls, also have laughing calls. This cassette clearly records the whooping, triumphant character of the herring gull's laugh, the more nasal, sarcastic laugh of the lesser black-back, and the great black-back's deep, croaking laughter. The black-headed gull does not laugh in this way, but has its own distinctive screeching cry, also recorded.

Other seabirds included on this tape are skuas, puffins, gannets and cormorants. There are now seven of these cassettes obtainable from Waxwing Associates, Little Okeford, Christchurch Road, Tring, Hertfordshire HP23 4EF (01422 823356).

In recent years, herring gulls have started nesting on rooftops, and have even settled in some inland towns, but most nests are found on cliff ledges overlooking the sea. The males hold a small territory, not round the nest-site as in most birds, but on the grassy clifftop above. They protect this space from other males, sometimes by fighting but most often by a strange display in which they pluck tufts of grass vigorously from around them. They do this so much that in some places they have caused erosion, and damage to the burrows in which puffins are nesting. They seem to need this territory for mating with the female.

Most pairs have young in the nest by early July, brown chicks that will be as big as the parents by early August. Once the young can fly, all the family will go off roaming, the mottled brown juveniles mixing with the pearly grey and white adults.

They are accomplished fishers, whether plunging from a height into the sea so that for a moment only their wingtips show above the surface, or swimming about and submerging their heads.

In the winter, their numbers are swollen by immigrants, and they spread across the country. Their wild laughter seems to be a challenge to rivals and a mating call. In the early days of spring, before they return to their cliffs, it will be echoing through the skies of Britain.

A name that has entered the bird-watcher's vocabulary in recent years is 'comic tern'. No such bird exists: the phrase is an abbreviation of 'common or arctic tern'. These two species are hard to distinguish when you get only a distant glimpse, and 'comic' conveniently covers them both.

Both species are summer visitors to Britain, the arctic terns nesting mainly in the north and west, the common terns more widely round the coasts and at a few places inland.

They are a beautiful race of birds, sometimes called 'sea-swallows' because of their forked tails with long streamers. They are mainly white and grey, like seagulls, but have a light, rising-and-falling motion as they patrol above the sea, looking down for fish.

The two species often nest together, on sand and shingle, or sometimes, in the case of the arctic terns, on thin turf on a cliff top. Like many species of tern, they both have black caps in summer, and the only obvious difference between them is the colour of their beaks. The common tern has a scarlet beak with a black tip; the arctic's is a pure blood-red.

When they have eggs or young, their beaks can be even more bloody, because they will swoop down, screaming, at a human intruder, and peck him hard on the scalp. Alternatively, they will drop a stream of liquid faeces on him. I put up the hood on my jacket when I was looking at some nestling arctic terns a few years ago, and it is still neatly bisected by a white line.

Terns compete with herring gulls for the nest-sites in some areas, and on the Isle of May the unfortunate gulls have been culled to give the terns a better chance. In early July the terns mostly have young that have wandered away from the nest but still cannot fly – rather podgy, ugly birds. They will be fledged by the end of the month.

The arctic terns will be the first to leave. This species makes the longest migratory flight of all the birds in the world. Some of them spend the summer around the pack-ice in the Arctic, and for our winter go down as far as the pack-ice in the Antarctic.

The common terns drift off more slowly, to winter along the west coast of Africa. They are often seen along rivers, or over lakes and reservoirs, as they head south.

There are two other species of tern that are fairly common breeders in this country, the little tern and the sandwich tern. The little tern is no bigger than a blackbird, and I find it particularly attractive, lively but approachable. It has a black cap but also a white forehead, and a yellow beak. You quite often see one, or a pair, flying to and fro off a bathing beach, calling with sharp cries, and hovering on quick-moving wings before diving. They nest in rather more scattered colonies, and often choose holiday beaches, which has done them some harm.

Sandwich terns nest in the common tern colonies and among black-headed gulls. They are easily distinguished: they are larger than the common terns, they have black beaks with yellow tips, and their black caps end in a rakish crest at the back of the head. Their nestlings are quite different, with noticeably hairy or spiky down.

That leaves, among British nesting terns, the roseate tern. It is the least common, nesting only on a few islands. But it is an especial thrill to see one because of its rarity and because it is such an exquisite bird: its beak black, its forked tail even longer than those of the 'comic' terns and (as its name suggests) its whole body suffused with a delicate pink in summer.

Puffins are puffing: the adults have a great deal of work to do in July. Most have to feed only one fat chick, which sits impatiently at the end of a long burrow, but they may bring it as many as 20 sand eels or sprats on a visit.

If you go just now to one of the Scottish islands or grassy headlands where they breed, you will find it either half-empty, or absolutely crowded with these upright little birds strutting to and fro. The reason for the varying number is because the puffins like to go out and fish together, and to come back together. Each gives a signal to the others when it is ready to set out, by dropping from the cliffs with a slow, moth-like flight.

Puffin

By mid-July, they no longer bother to feed their chick when they return, but just dump fish in the mouth of the burrow.

The adult puffins prepared these burrows in May, either by taking over rabbit holes, or digging one for themselves with their sharp toenails. In time, a breeding area may become so honeycombed with their burrows that the whole topsoil, with its pink thrift and grass, just collapses. This happened on the Welsh island of Grassholm, eight miles west of Skomer, Dyfed, where there were three-quarters of a million puffins in 1890, and where now the species is extinct. However, there are still plenty in northern waters. There are eight to ten million pairs in Iceland, and in Britain they are holding their own with almost half a million pairs, most of them in the Outer Hebrides. One must be glad of that, because they are unique birds, with their red and blue triangular beaks and their sad-looking eyes.

The young will emerge later this month, and make a cautious night flight down to the sea. Even then, they may be snapped up in the moonlight by great black-backed gulls.

After that it will not be long before the adults lose the coloured adornments on their beaks, and the whole colony sets out for the oceans. Then only seafarers will see them, until that day in March when the first gaudy spring puffin hurtles in and starts looking for its burrow again.

William Shakespeare would have seen red kites scavenging in the London streets, and until the end of the eighteenth century they were common in Britain. But Victorian gamekeepers put an end to that and, until recently, only a few pairs lingered on in the Welsh hills.

Now there is a chance of seeing them all over Britain

again. In 1989, five red kites were released in southern England and five in Scotland, in the wooded-valley terrain that they favour. The Scottish birds had been taken from nests in Sweden, the English ones from nests in Spain.

This was a project set up by the Royal Society for the Protection of Birds and the Joint Nature Conservation Committee. They went on releasing red kites for the following five years, until they had reached a total of 93 birds in England, and the same number north of the border.

The success of the project has been remarkable. In winter now, red kites are reported soaring over the land in numerous parts of Scotland, and in England from the West Country to the east coast. Startled motorists sometimes see them flapping up from the edge of the M40. Many pairs have bred successfully. In England at the end of 1994, the total number of red kites had climbed to 128. In Scotland, where there has been a higher death rate, there were 74.

The red kite is a wonderful bird to see, and totally distinctive, with its deeply forked, rusty-red tail, its rufous body, its pale head and the striking white patch under its wings.

Last year I watched one circling over a hillside. Suddenly a crow flew up at it, and I had a magnificent view of the kite wheeling and swerving, steering languidly with its tail, as it shook the crow off. Later I saw it foraging with many twists and turns over some rough pasture.

The kites feed mainly on carrion – rabbits that have died of myxomatosis, dead sheep, dead birds. They are quite often flushed from roads where they have been picking up animals killed by cars. In a year or two, some of the breeding sites will be made public. Meanwhile, the possibility of seeing one in the sky adds a thrill to any bird-watching day.

At the beginning of January, I wrote about the thousands of wild swans on the Ouse Washes, that strange, beautiful terrain that lies between the fenland canals on the Cambridge–Norfolk border. Most of the swans are now far away, breeding in the Arctic.

What other birds can be found on the Washes six months on? Much of the flooded land has reverted to meadow for the summer, and the really spectacular birds of this season are the black-tailed godwits. They are tall, handsome waders that walk about in the remaining pools on their long legs, dipping their heads beneath the water and probing for food. But they need dry land for nesting, and sometimes breed on the Washes. They can often be seen from the hides at Welney, Norfolk, where the Wildfowl and Wetlands Trust has its centre.

Lapwings and redshanks now have practically full-grown young. The lapwings fly from the fields to the muddy edges of the pools with a slow, wobbling motion. The redshanks speed from one feeding-place to another on slim wings with silver trailing edges, and when they settle, they walk about delicately on their bright red legs. Both species will soon be forming loose flocks and moving away, the redshanks mainly going down to the coast. There are also one or two greenshanks about – larger, paler birds than the redshanks, with an upturned bill and green legs.

Snipe also breed in the meadows, but they have not done so well yet: they are later breeders than the other common waders, and sometimes their nests get washed out in the June rains.

There are also plenty of small birds in this watery countryside. Along the edges of the rivers and canals, you see a yellow wagtail every few hundred yards, sitting on a fence or on a thistle with its tail bouncing up and down. With their yellow underparts and greenish backs, and their quick, undulating flight, they seem like the spirit of the water meadows. They have a short, sweeping call, recognizable from a long way off. Pied wagtails are also common on the canal banks.

Hundreds of swifts hurtle past, screaming, as you walk along the canal banks. Sand martins twist and turn above the water, as they have done since time immemorial. A vertical cliff of sand was dug out not far from the centre a few years ago and was immediately discovered by sand martins, who burrowed out nest-holes in it.

The landscape is lush now – swathes of purple loosestrife grow at the edge of the water, the sallows and osiers are dense with leaf, the reeds are tall. Young sedge and reed warblers are hiding in places like these, with their parents still feeding them. A hobby occasionally swoops across the lagoon: house and sand martins are favourite prey, and it can catch them on the wing.

Pied Wagtail

There are two or three months of abundant food ahead for the yellow wagtails and the warblers, the swifts and swallows and martins. The adults will have time to recuperate from the labours of breeding, and the young will have time and leisure to grow up. But by the time the wild swans return, and the meadows have vanished under chill water, these species will be very far away.

In the latter part of July, the fields grow more silent. The whitethroats that sang in the hedges are busy looking after their young; in the field-side spinneys, the willow warbler's cadences ripple out more rarely from the dark foliage, and the robin's song begins to falter. Occasionally, an anxious whitethroat peers out from a thick maple hedge and you get a glimpse of its wonderful silver throat.

You hear only three birds singing regularly now as you walk among ripening wheat: the skylark, the corn bunting and the yellowhammer. In the prevailing silence, the skylarks seem even finer singers than in the spring. First, one goes up from almost underfoot, with a few rippling calls; as it climbs, it begins to pour out an unbroken flow of lyrical song, with some throbbing passages as intense as a nightingale's. Another flutters up into the air not far away and starts to sing. Suddenly you hear a third in the sky further across the fields. Their voices seem to fold into each other like the petals of a poppy.

Of course, they are not performing a Mozartian trio: they are asserting their claim to the patch of field below them, where they have eggs or young. They fight their musical battles high above their family's heads. Through the field-glasses you find that they are staying almost still in the air by facing the wind and flying into it at wind speed.

When they stop singing, they drop down like lead, halting their descent with a flicker of their wings only a few yards from the ground. There, I always think, they look like small game birds, with their streaky brown plumage and their way of running rapidly along a field path or through a thin patch of corn. What makes them unmistakable is the little pointed crest on their head.

Corn buntings, too, like to sing above the fields: they find the highest perch they can, and particularly favour cables running between electricity pylons. They have a thin, weird song that is audible a long way off: it begins with a few sharp chirps, then breaks into a loud metallic jangle that has been compared to the rattle of a bunch of large keys.

Sometimes you see one sitting on a wire next to a yellowhammer (also a bunting), and that brings out what a stocky bird the corn bunting is, with its thick bull neck. The yellowhammer is slimmer; a much more colourful bird, with its primrose-yellow head and breast, though the corn bunting has quite elegantly patterned brown plumage. The male corn bunting sings with its head back and beak wide open: it looks as if it is snarling. It often has several mates, nesting under hedges or at the foot of a field thistle, and it keeps an eye on them all. Corn buntings are distributed erratically in the countryside: in the rolling, chalky fields of Hertfordshire, for instance, you can come across five in a mile and then no more for a long way.

The yellowhammers are also still singing in the hedges – a patient repetition, hour after hour, of their little run of chinking notes with a long 'cheee' at the end of it. Now and then a wren bursts out breathlessly in an elder; a late blackcap mutters a few musical notes from a wild rose bush.

But these are not the songs of spring. The wheat will be harvested and silence will dominate the land in the long afternoons of high summer.

The shelduck is one of the oddest of our birds. And in late July it behaves very oddly indeed. Most of the shelducks from Britain and many from the Continent are going off on a moult migration.

They gather in enormous numbers on the islands in the Heligoland Bight off the north-west German coast, where they feel secure and can find plenty of food. There they will stay until October, by which time they will be in shining new plumage.

However, there is a problem. The young from this year's nests are still not fledged. Some of them are half-grown, some are still ducklings clothed in rather pretty, marbled down. What to do about those? The answer is that some shelducks stay behind and look after large crèches of young birds. You can see them now on the estuaries – long lines of small shelducks waddling clumsily across the wet sand behind a pompous-looking adult.

They are odd birds in other ways. They are something between a duck and a goose, and in fact belong to a group called sheldgeese. The 'sheld' part of their name means 'pied' and they are indeed boldly variegated birds, one of the easiest of all species to identify.

They have dark, glossy green heads, white bodies with black along the back of the wing, and a chestnut band like some mayoral badge of office across their chests. The drake's self-important demeanour is further increased in summer by the growth of a large red knob at the base of his beak, and the development of a black belly.

They fly like geese, in skeins or wedges, and with quite slow wing beats, unlike the fast, whinnying flight of ducks. Most of the time they are sociable birds, although solitary individuals often turn up on inland lakes in July and August during migration. These strays look very bizarre, floating about on the water among the coots and the moulting mallards.

Most of the young birds began their life in rabbit holes along sandy shores, which is where shelducks prefer to nest. They also nest under haystacks or even in deserted huts – four nests were found some years ago on the floor of a shepherd's shed. The nest is lined with soft down from the female's breast, and the eggs, which may number as many as 15 in one clutch, are creamy-white.

Sometimes two females will lay in the same nest, producing a small mountain of eggs. The females need to build up a great deal of energy to lay so many eggs, and when they are feeding during this period, the drake will guard them assiduously to make sure they are not interrupted.

By now all that business of laying and incubating is over, and whether they are on their native coasts or up in the Heligoland Bight the shelducks will have an easy summer. They like to feed on the ebb tide, sieving the water or the liquid mud with their beaks in search of the sea snails for which they have a special taste.

Shelduck

On stiller water they will 'up-end' to feed, with only their tails and the tips of their wings showing above the water: when a whole party of them is doing this they look like an encampment of little tents on the sea. The young birds will dive in pursuit of prey, but they give that up as they get bigger.

In October, the British shelducks will be back again, reunited with their young and the duckling-minders, though they will probably not recognize each other. Many shelducks from other countries will come with them. Throughout the winter, they will form a quaint and colourful band of birds round our coastline.

The quail eggs one often wolfs down at cocktail parties these days, and the little birds that appear regularly on restaurant tables, come from quail farms both here and on the Continent. The wild bird has been rare for a long time and is thoroughly protected by law.

Occasionally, however, we get an influx of quails, often quite late in the summer. Considerable numbers were recorded in 1989 and in 1995 almost 1,000 were heard calling in the wheatfields and the long hay. Yorkshire was particularly favoured, with about 25 calling birds in the Derwent valley.

I say 'calling birds' because these little creatures are not often seen. They announce their presence with a triple whistle, commonly transcribed as 'wet-mi-lips'. They pipe up from the depths of the corn at dusk and dawn. When they are disturbed, they prefer to run rather than fly, and it is usually a dog that persuades one of them to take wing, and gives the dog's owner a chance of seeing it whirr away. It is like a small, sandy partridge, with dark markings on the head.

Many of the 1995 birds arrived in late June and July, and there is an interesting theory about this. It is suspected that quails often have a first brood in the spring in North Africa, where the weed seeds provide an abundant food supply before the weather gets too hot and dry. Then they fly north, and have a second brood later in the summer in Europe.

Alternatively, it has been suggested that the young birds which grew up in North Africa in early spring do not wait, like most birds, till the following year to breed, but fly north when they are fledged and nest in the same summer.

If either of these speculations is correct, some of the late 1995 arrivals may well have bred here. This is in addition to the handful of pairs that come every year in the spring, and are found mainly in the rolling, chalky cornfields of Wiltshire and Dorset.

The hot weather in southern Europe, and the south-east winds, no doubt were responsible for the appearance of the later birds seen in 1995.

The quails' nests are small, grass-lined hollows in the corn or hay, and they lay up to a dozen eggs – creamy with blotches, as the gourmets know. One extraordinary fact has been discovered about the young birds while they are still in the egg: they start calling before they hatch out, and they listen to each other in their shells. This enables them to co-ordinate their hatching.

Although the eggs are laid over a period of several days, the young all emerge within a period of about six hours. It is important to each of them that they should do this, because as soon as they dry out they leave the nest – and if one gets left behind it is likely to lose its parents and die.

It is possible that the quail will become common here again. The great spring slaughter of quails for food in southern Europe has been curbed by legislation, and new initiatives to help farmland birds in Britain, such as the RSPB's 'skylark appeal' may help quails, too. It would be good if country children once again knew the cry in the fields of 'wet-mi-lips'.

AUGUST

Coming suddenly on a lonely pool on moor or farmland, you may be surprised in early August to see a black-and-white bird fly up with a loud, piping cry. The white is on the bird's rump, which makes it look like a large, long-winged house martin. You have stumbled across one of the first autumn migrants, a green sandpiper.

Not many birds are on the move yet, but green sandpipers generally lead the great flight south. They summer in wet woods in the north-eastern parts of Europe – Sweden, Finland, Russia. Most wading birds nest on the ground, but these have the surprising habit of using old thrushes' nests in alder trees.

I have just been watching three of them feeding together in a muddy pool in Hertfordshire, all of them wading up to their stomachs. Oddly enough, although they seem quite dramatically black-and-white when they go up, they look brown when you get a good view of them.

Why are they called 'green'? I saw the answer to that as the sun caught their plumage from time to time at different angles: they had a distinctly green sheen. When their legs are visible, these can be seen to be green, too.

There are other intimations of the migrations to come. Curlews are appearing on the estuaries as they descend from the moors, and lapwings are beginning to shift about all over Europe. Meanwhile, cuckoos are disappearing silently from woods and fields.

However, most of the smaller summer visitors are still around their nesting places.

August is the teenage month for birds. There are millions of juveniles lurking in the foliage or in the heather, or floating out on the sea, all of them just about to moult and assume the feathers of adulthood.

Most of them spend a certain amount of time with the adults before they become independent. But in one or two species, they never have any contact with their parents after they have left the nest. Young swifts suddenly fly out from under the eaves where they grew up, and young puffins leave their burrows at night – and their parents come back with food for them, only to find that they have gone for ever.

However, that is not the typical pattern. By contrast, young sand martins learn to recognize the individual voices of their parents before they leave the holes in the sandbanks where they spend their first days of life. If they did not do that, they would never find their parents in the swirl of birds around the quarry – and they need them, because they are not yet ready to feed themselves.

Just now you can find many families of birds still together in the trees. Thin cries in the tops of the limes and the poplars reveal a little party of spotted flycatchers. They are summer visitors that arrive later than other birds, and in most cases the second brood has only just flown. Sometimes they move off to a churchyard, where you can see the adults and the young all sitting on separate gravestones, darting out for flies.

Goldfinches have two or even three broods in a year, so there are plenty of family parties of those about. The young birds chase their parents through the sky, making loud, bell-like twitters, and when they all land in a hawthorn bush, the youngsters flap their gold-barred wings like mad to encourage their parents to produce some insects. It is like a small electric storm among the ripening berries.

The young goldfinches lack the brilliant red, white and black faces of their parents – and indeed many young birds have comparatively dull plumage. It has been suggested that this protects them if they stray into another territory. Male territory holders attack intruders that have the full adult plumage. Robins, for instance, attack other robins with red breasts – but they are indifferent to the spotty brown breasts of juvenile robins.

One place which is a particular magnet for different species at present is a large puddle. One hot day I sat down, half-concealed, near a puddle on a woodland path. Titmice kept swooping over it from one side to the other, but a blackbird was the first to settle and walk into the water. It kept dipping its head forward so that its shoulders touched the water, then shivered its wings so that the drops flew all over its upper parts.

Three young blue tits suddenly landed all together at the edge of the puddle. They did not venture beyond the stones and debris in the shallows, but they managed to give themselves a quick bath before all flying nervously away.

It was clear how much birds need to wash their dusty feathers on hot, dry days. Those readers who help birds to survive a cold spell in winter by putting out food for them can do equally good service by providing a shallow vessel with water for them to bathe in on hot days.

The turtle dove is one of those birds that is more often heard than seen. In early August you can still hear it making its soft purring notes in hedgerows in the Midlands and southern England. Its Latin name is *turtur,* and that word mimics the bird's sound very well.

There was a time when our fox terrier would always bark when the telephone rang, and once I heard him start up when a turtle dove began singing outside the window. He had perceived that the rhythm of the song, and even to some extent its timbre, is very like the 'brr-brr' of a phone.

The old English name was simply 'turtle', and the bird appears in a famous verse of the Bible in Coverdale's translation of the Song of Solomon: 'The flowers appear on the earth; the time of the singing of birds is come, and the voice of the turtle is heard in our land.' Here, that would have to refer to the month of May, since the turtle dove is one of the later summer visitors to arrive from Africa. In fact, it is the only migratory British dove or pigeon (those are alternative names, incidentally, for birds who belong to one family). The others – the woodpigeon, stock dove, rock dove and collared dove – sing more or less all the year round.

The turtle dove is a beautiful bird, with its dappled orange-brown back, pink breast and grey head. It has a small black-and-white mark on its neck, and a black tail with white edges. It is smaller and more slender than the fat woodpigeon.

As with other pigeons, the male has a display flight with which it courts its mate, climbing up into the air, then gliding and spiralling down, and singing again as soon as it lands. The mated pair have become a symbol for amorous lovers – 'a right pair of turtle doves' – since they sit on a branch pressed up against each other, rubbing bills, and preening each other around the nape. They nest in bushes and hedges, making a fairly rickety platform of twigs. They lay two white eggs, which you can sometimes see from beneath through cracks in the platform, and both members of the pair take turns to incubate them.

The young birds in the nest are fed at first on 'pigeon's milk', a curd-like substance that is formed in their parents' crops. Within days, they have turned into a fearsome spectacle. They have long, straggly yellowish down, flat heads and a fierce-looking beak. If you push your head through the twigs to study their appearance, they snap and hiss at you. However, after three weeks in the nest, when they are ready to fly, they have come to resemble their placid-looking parents, apart from lacking the mark on the neck.

The first fledglings are out and about now, and the adults are nesting again. One particular summer flower attracts them as food – the pink-flowered fumitory, a weed of the cornfields, of which they eat the seeds. The name 'fumitory' comes from the Latin *fumus terrae*, or 'smoke of the earth', because it was once thought to grow without seeds. Like many other cornfield plants, it has grown rarer because of the farmers' use of herbicides.

Turtle doves have also declined in numbers over the past 20 years, from 125,000 breeding pairs to about 75,000. Loss of hedgerows has no doubt played its part in that decline, as well as loss of food plants.

But the turtle dove has always been a victim. It is one of the favourite targets of the Mediterranean 'sportsmen' who go out shooting in the autumn. The bags of migrating turtle doves have always been particularly high in Greece, and the slaughter goes on in spite of all attempts to legislate against it.

Meanwhile, oddly enough, a close relative of the turtle dove, the collared dove, has established itself as a common bird in Western Europe. When this visitor from the Middle East first bred in Britain in 1955 it was called the 'collared turtle dove', but it has now lost the 'turtle' from its name. This is right, because its song is not in the least like its relative's – it is a loud triple note, 'coo-*coo*-coo' heard from church towers and television aerials.

The two species scarcely see each other in the summer,

since the collared doves like village or even town life, while the turtle doves keep resolutely out among the fields and farms. But they come together to forage in the autumn stubble fields – or at least in those fields where any grain or weed seeds are left. If you find them together, you can distinguish them quite easily: the collared doves look like grey ghosts among the colourful turtles of old England.

The moors are noisy after 12 August. Grouse shooting has begun and the guns are banging as the birds go up or come over. But bird-watchers see the red grouse in very different circumstances. Most often they startle them in the heather; the birds speed off with a clattering cry and rapid wing beats, then glide, landing again as much as a mile away. They go downwind, and often swerve and tilt from side to side – 'jinking' – as they fly.

For much of the spring and summer the birds can be heard calling on the moors, but you are likely to get the best views of them through field-glasses across a valley or loch. Their cackles and crowings echo across the water, then suddenly you will see one or two running about on the hillside. They have reddish-brown feathers with bold markings, the male with a red wattle over the eye, but they look black at this distance.

The males fly up from the heather in brief song-flights: they make barking notes when they are in the air and give their best-known call, the ringing 'go-back, go-back' when they land. They have brisk fights, and sometimes chase their mate across a bare patch of territory.

At one time it was thought that the red grouse was a wholly British species. Now, it is accepted that it is just a distinctive sub-species of the willow grouse, or willow ptarmigan, and

Red Grouse

that there are no birds found exclusively in the British Isles. The willow grouse differs in having white wing-feathers in summer and in turning white, except for a black tail, in winter.

The grouse nest in a hollow in the heather; they generally lay 6 to 11 eggs with chocolate-brown blotches – in some years many clutches are ruined by snow. The young birds leave the nest as soon as they hatch, and hide in the heather, but they can fly after 12 days. Heather is vital to their lives: they need old, deep heather to nest in, and young, growing heather in order to eat the shoots.

The numbers of red grouse have decreased in recent years, mainly due to poor management of the moors. For the grouse to flourish, stretches of heather need to be burnt in rotation, so that there is a steady supply of new shoots as it grows again. In hard weather they may leave the moors to look for grain, or even fly up into hawthorns for the berries.

There is even more to see and share while looking for

grouse. You may spot meadow pipits. They often continue nesting into August, and you will usually see a few males overhead, climbing and swooping in their own modest song-flight. Others will be perched on a fence or a tall spray of heather with a beak full of insects, waiting for a chance to go down to their young hidden in a nest under a tussock. They are pretty little streaky brown birds and very common – more the spirit of the moors, for me, than the grouse.

There may be a few curlews about, but by mid-August you are more likely to hear their wild song on the estuaries where they have gone to spend the coming winter. In valleys with a few bushes there is a chance of seeing ring ouzels, which look like blackbirds with white throats: but they too are on the move across Britain, heading towards the Mediterranean. Buzzards and ravens may drift through the sky, hoping to spot carrion.

The shooting will be over by mid-December. By then, the remaining grouse – and there are always plenty – will have started gathering in flocks, or 'packs'. Winter is generally hard on the moors, and the foxes will be prowling. But in the first days of spring, the grouse's firm challenge –'go-back, go-back' — will be heard once more over the withered heather flowers.

The third week of August is exactly the week to go looking for hobbies – and there is more chance of finding them than there was a few years ago. Hobbies are small falcons that visit Britain from May to September. They like open downland with clumps of pine trees, but are also found in undisturbed farmland, as long as there are old trees in hedges to provide nesting-sites.

They are geniuses on the wing. They pursue small birds,

and also dragonflies and beetles, at breakneck speed. They can pick up swallows and house martins in the air, and will sometimes even catch a flying swift.

They have slaty-blue backs, and that is really all you see of them when they are dashing away from you along a river, rocketing from side to side. Overhead, with their sickle-shaped wings, they look like large swifts. If you get a view of one perching in a treetop, you see a hooked beak, a fierce-looking moustache, a streaky breast, and some rusty red around the thighs.

Once they begin nesting, they are silent and cunning. They contrive to approach their nest and to leave it almost invisibly. I know a good bird-watcher who had some hobbies nesting at the end of his garden, and who knew nothing about them until the young were fledged.

They never build their own nest, but use an old crow's nest or squirrel's drey. They breed late, for a good reason. They have two or three handsome eggs with rich, reddish-brown spots, which are laid in mid-June. These hatch in mid-July, and the fledglings are ready to leave the nest in mid-August. That means that the young hobbies are being fed just when the young swallows and house martins are out in the skies, inexperienced and plentiful. The adult hobbies cause havoc among them. It is also the time of year when plenty of darter and hawker dragonflies are coming out of the water and drying their wings.

And why is mid-August a good time to look for hobbies? It is because it is the only time of year when the hobbies call a lot. The adults have a 'kee-kee-kee' note, like a rather melancholy version of the kestrel's call, and also a screaming, wailing cry. Both can be heard from a long way off, and both are much in use as warning calls when the young are growing large in the nest, or just after they leave it. If you hear these plangent sounds in the distance and follow them up, you may discover one or both of the parents circling overhead.

The young are also noisy when they have flown and, once you have detected the presence of a family, with patience you should be able to find them high in the trees. Compared with their parents, they are remarkably tame, peering down at you with sharp eyes over their moustaches.

Twenty-five years ago there were probably only 100 to 200 pairs of hobbies each year in Britain, most of them on heathland in the south. Now there appear to be 700 or 800 pairs, and they have extended their range to Wales, Shropshire and Derbyshire, with even a few in North Yorkshire. So it is time to hunt the hunter – even if you cannot do it with all the speed and dash of the bird you are seeking.

Tourists taking the water-taxi from Marco Polo airport to Venice often remark on the exquisite white herons feeding along the mainland shore. They are tall, elegant birds, with black beaks and legs, and in the summer have two long plumes on their head. With a better view, one can also see downy plumes half-floating on their backs. They are little egrets – and the feathers on their backs are the *aigrettes* that milliners once used for trimming hats.

Until recently they were very rare birds in Britain, with just an occasional vagrant being recorded here at intervals of many years. But suddenly they have become more common – a very welcome contrast to the decline of many species here in the last decade or so. For several years now, in August, they have been reported along the south coast, mainly in Devon, Dorset and Sussex. Particularly good places for watching them have been the Teign estuary and Poole harbour.

Little Egret

What seems to have happened is that they have been extending their breeding area up the west side of France. So some young egrets from the new French breeding sites have been wandering north across the channel on to our shores.

An even more exciting prospect is that they may become regular breeding birds. These young egrets travel for two reasons – to find good feeding places for a while before they are obliged by the weather to turn south again, and also to prospect for possible nesting places in the following year. There may be no room for them in their parents' breeding colonies, if large numbers of young have survived the winter – so it will be greatly to their advantage that they have scouted around already. On the whole, though, the little egrets in the more northern parts of their range go south again in September and winter along the Mediterranean, where they join up with the greater part of the European breeding population.

They are sociable birds, but very silent during the winter months. Once nesting time comes, the picture is very different. I have seen the nesting colonies on the Nile dam above Cairo. Hundreds of pairs of birds build bulky nests together in the waterside trees, with buff-backed herons side by side with the little egrets. A perpetual din of snorts and groans and croakings comes from the settlement. They are quite tame in the trees, and there is no difficulty in distinguishing the two species.

Compared with the little egrets, the buff-backed herons are squat, hunchbacked birds. They have yellow beaks, and at this time of the year have a pinkish-brown flush on their heads and backs, whereas the little egrets have totally white plumage. You can also see that the buff-backed herons have reddish legs, while the black legs of the little egrets give way to yellow feet.

Although they nest together, the two species are less often seen feeding in the same place. The buff-backed herons, which are also known as cattle egrets, like to go into the fields and feed among the cows: visitors to southern Spain know them well. However, the little egrets stay near water.

If we get one or two pairs of these wonderful creatures nesting here in the next few years we shall have something to rejoice over. And – who knows? – one day we shall perhaps have whole squealing, grunting colonies of them, waving their plumes in our willow trees.

There are few finer sights than a cock pheasant standing at the edge of a wood and trumpeting. In the sunlight, its head and neck are a glittering green, and its body glows like bronze. It is adorned with ear-tufts, red wattles round its eyes, and a white neckband. It presses its long, barred tail to

Pheasant

the ground, flaps its wings a couple of times, sends its double call ringing across the fields, then flaps its wings vigorously again. It is inviting hen birds to join its harem, and warning off other cock pheasants.

The bird has been doing this in Britain since Norman times, and possibly since the Romans were here, but until the late eighteenth century, there was one difference: it did not have the white neckband. The 'British pheasant', as it is sometimes called, was brought from the Caucasus, and lacked this ornament. In the last quarter of the eighteenth century, a closely related sub-species, the Chinese ring-necked pheasant, was introduced. It quickly interbred with the old immigrants and now it is rare to see a cock pheasant without the Chinese bird's white collar. Pheasants still crow throughout much of Asia, in their native woods and reed-beds.

The cock pheasants have several mates – much dowdier birds, with shorter tails, who do all the work of incubating the eggs and caring for the young. They each lay about a dozen creamy-brown eggs on a scrape in the ground. I remember once flushing a hen pheasant from a nest in a spectacular setting – under magnificent royal ferns in a wood on the Scottish island of Gigha. She exploded out of the ferns under our feet, scattering some of the eggs. Doubtless she would have reassembled them later, but we did it for her, and left them neatly in the hollow under its handsome canopy.

In August the woods and cornfields are full of young pheasants. You detect them in the ripening wheat by their strange squeals or the shaking of the ears of corn. If you come across one in long grass, it stretches its head out and then runs like mad.

Pheasants mostly prefer to use their legs rather than fly: they never migrate, and generally spend their whole life in the same small area. But they have flight muscles that enable them to rise quickly when they need to, after which they glide away over the bracken or through the tree-trunks, then land and start running. In the evening, they use their wings again when they fly up on to the branches of trees to roost. The fox is a deadly enemy to them, and they are out of its way up there.

Large numbers of pheasants have a more artificial life than this. Though they hardly ever live wholly in captivity, many are rounded up by gamekeepers in the early spring and kept in safe areas to breed. Their eggs are collected and hatched in an incubator, and the young birds are then set free.

Many of the sprinting youngsters you come across just now started life in a gamekeeper's incubator. They forage in the wild, or glean any food, such as maize, that might be put down for them.

When fully grown, the cock bird will be as much as 3ft long, of which more than half will be the length of its tail.

Many millions of pheasants will be roaming the countryside in the next few months. Until the end of September they will be able to enjoy the autumn fruits in peace. Then, on 1 October, the shooting will begin. Game experts have estimated that only about half of the young birds released into the wild are shot in the three months of the season. But as winter wears on, many other pheasants, both young and old, are killed by predators or succumb to disease.

By next spring the numbers will have fallen to very much what they were last spring. The cock birds will be dividing up the woodlands and crowing out their defiant and amorous calls once more, and the cycle of life and death which draws man and bird together will be starting again.

SEPTEMBER

What Victorian ornithologists called the 'great south flight' is well under way by the first week of September. Millions of birds are moving south across Europe. The numbers are quite extraordinary. With ranks swelled by the summer's young, it is calculated that 900 million willow warblers are on the move, 220 million swallows, 90 million house martins.

But where are they all? That is another of the wonders of the autumn migration. In spring, the arrival of the summer visitors is obvious because they take up territories and sing. In autumn, birds such as waders are noticeable on the shore; but most of the small birds slip away virtually unseen.

Yet if you are alert, you can sometimes detect them. Willow warblers are everywhere in the deep foliage just now; you can find them by their soft 'hweet' call, and then, if you wait, one is sure to appear for a moment on another twig of the hawthorn or elder, bright green in its autumn plumage. Its close relative, the chiffchaff, is one of the most noticeable of all of these southward-drifting passerines, because it sings on migration, and its ringing 'chiff-chaff, chiff-chaff' sounds out from treetops in parks and gardens for an hour or two before it moves on.

However, other warblers, such as the innumerable blackcaps, whitethroats and sedge warblers that nested here, make very little noise. For one thing, they are all very busy feeding as they travel along. Those birds, such as the whitethroat, that are heading south of the Sahara, will eventually have to fly 1,000 km across the Mediterranean and 1,500km across the desert before they can stop for food.

In the early, slower stages of their journey, they often move on in the early morning, and they can sometimes be spotted from hilltops.

In London, observers watching carefully from high buildings do sometimes see small parties of migrating birds flying overhead. Skylarks make sweet, liquid calls as they fly, so they draw attention to themselves. Chaffinches fly very high, many of them out of sight to the unaided eye.

The best time for watching city skies is in the first few hours of daylight, though it is known that migrants are on the move at all hours. On a clear night, they are often seen as fleeting black shapes passing across the face of the moon.

There are several places on the south coast where the the migrants concentrate before setting off across the Channel, notably Portland Bill in Dorset and Dungeness in Kent. Here the bushes are alive with skulking birds, not to mention bird-watchers.

How did birds come to live like this? Current opinion favours the idea that it all began after the Ice Age. Birds were already abundant in the tropical zones, but as the ice began to retreat northward, vast tracts of land opened up, with no avian inhabitants, and rich feeding in the summer months. So birds began to move into those territories. Those that flew back in winter survived; those that stayed died. Gradually, in some species, the habit of migration evolved as a set pattern.

In fact, in certain species the pattern set unnecessarily hard. Wheatears winter in Africa and in the summer fly north to Europe. Many of them then turn east across Russia and fly as far as Alaska. But those birds do not migrate directly south when autumn comes. They fly west, and once more down through Europe, following the route that they evolved so many millennia ago.

As for how they find their way, that is far from being fully understood. There is evidence for navigation by the sun and stars, and even for a response in birds to the earth's magnetic field, as well as for the straightforward following of a coastline or other visible landmarks. At the moment, scientists think that birds make a complicated use of all these methods. Invisible creatures, travelling by unknown means: that is the somehow rather cheering picture that bird migration still presents.

On the door of St Bega's church, on the shores of Bassenthwaite Lake in Cumbria, there is a notice: 'Please close the door because of the swallows.' Swallows dive confidently in and out of the barn doors, but if they swoop into a church looking for somewhere to nest they can get trapped when they try to fly out again through the high windows.

There are plenty of them about in the Lake District in September. Where the sheep are drifting through long grass, the swallows sweep to and fro in front of them, picking up the flying insects that the sheep have disturbed. The birds have insignificant beaks, but they have a wide gape, and they just gulp down the insects as they sweep through the air. Occasionally, though, they make use of their beaks: one has been recorded sitting by a spider's web and picking up the flies as they got caught in it.

Most of the young birds are now out of the nest, and they form a large proportion of the loose groups that constantly move round the fields and farms looking for good hunting grounds. When you watch them flying round you, the young seem to be as deft on the wing as their parents, but they are probably not. They have not yet grown the long feathers either side of the tail that the adults tilt for ultra-fine control when they swerve in pursuit of a fly.

High in the sky, they twitter all the time, and when alarmed they make loud chinking cries. They will mob a sparrow-hawk if it appears on the scene, and drive it away.

Swallows do not have much competition for their food, though I have seen a spotted flycatcher sitting in a gnarled old holly at the edge of a sheep pasture, darting out every now and again to catch insects while the swallows flashed past. Fortunately there were no collisions.

In some barns you can still hear young birds murmuring in their nest high in the rafters, because the swallow nests late and has two or even three broods. Young from earlier broods, and adults that have finished nesting, are beginning to gather now on telephone wires. This sociable habit seems to bind them together as a flock before they set off on their very long migration south.

Their winter home is in southern Africa, and it is thought that they originated there, only acquiring the habit of migrating north in our summer about 15,000 years ago as the Ice Age glaciers retreated. The warming of Europe opened up new territories with abundant food, but only those which turned south again in the autumn survived. The last swallows will not depart from Britain's shores until October or even later. So there is still plenty of time to look out for them in the sky, their twitters sprinkling down and their wings continually opening and closing, so that one moment they are fluttering, and the next looking like a darting blue arrow.

If you get up early, in the village of Cley on the Norfolk coast, you will see a strange sight most days in September. In the half-light of dawn, shadowy figures, well wrapped-up against the morning chill, are winding down the street. They have long, dark instruments resting on their shoulders, and remind you irresistibly of Brueghel's winter hunters setting out.

But these weapons are not guns, but telescopes; and the hunters are sea-watchers, heading for the high bank and the shingle to do a dawn watch for autumn migrants. Far out at sea they will hope to detect an arctic skua clipping the waves – a brown hawk of the oceans on its way south, after a summer spent harrying the gulls in their colonies and stealing their food. If the watchers are very lucky, they may see a great skua – a really hefty bird – or even a rare pomarine or a long-tailed skua. Bobbing among the waves there may be a black-necked grebe, a small intrepid diver into the choppy water.

The sea-watchers are hardy, devoted bird men and women, happy to sit there with their flask and sandwiches through long, barren hours. It is better for the more restless bird-watcher to go looking at waders, which are now flocking down the British coasts wherever the mud stretches out between sea and shore. The east coast has the greater numbers, because so many birds come in across the North Sea. Blakeney, a little north of Cley, is one of the many excellent places to be now.

At low tide there are broad mud flats covered with birds – but one must be careful venturing on to them. The tide comes in quickly by many channels. Once, when I was trying to get a closer view of a grey plover, I had to leap back fast over streams in the mud that were suddenly filling up behind me.

One can very easily be lured on by a grey plover, because it is such a beautiful bird. It has brilliant silvery upper parts

Grey Plover

separated by a white line from its black face and breast, and it positively gleams against a background of mud and seaweed. This is the summer plumage, which in many birds is now giving way to a duller silvery-grey all over; but in late August there are always some that have not yet changed colour. In flight, they are reasonably easy to identify because they have a conspicuous black 'armpit', and also a distinctive alarm call of three piping notes.

Many other waders are already present in large numbers, and passage will continue until October. The rippling cries of curlews can be heard at any time of day or night, and their portly figures can be seen probing in the distance at the water's edge. Ringed plovers run across the wet sand, then stand stock still; these small white-collared birds like to patter up and down with their orange legs to attract prey to the surface.

Dunlin are among the commonest of the waders: they are small sandpipers with chestnut backs, and a black belly if they still have their summer feathers. In some years, there is a considerable passage of curlew sandpipers, which are very like dunlin, but have the downcurved bill of the larger bird they are named after.

One migrant wader I particularly like is the ruff (or reeve, in the case of the female). In summer, the males have extraordinary black or orange feather-boas round their necks, but by now they are quite plain and modest-looking again. However, they are wonderfully delicate birds, moving gently through the shallow water on long reddish legs, with soft brown plumage that glows pink in the evening sun. They are among the most sympathetic characters in this play with a cast of millions that is currently being staged on our shores.

Sometimes you are driving along a country road when a whole dark ploughed field seems to rise into the air, and break up into black and silver. It is a flock of lapwings taking to the air. When they are standing, their dark backs can make them almost invisible. But most of their underwing is silvery white, and it flashes as they rise.

They go off with an oddly floppy flight, their round wings beating the air without much conviction. They will often just circle round, and come down again in ones or twos when the alarm – it might be a passing sparrow-hawk – is over.

Waves of lapwings come to Britain from northern Germany and Scandinavia in September, and throughout the winter, these flocks will be moving to and fro across the British countryside, now on the coast, now inland, to dodge icy weather.

Black-headed gulls that come into the fields in winter give them a great deal of trouble. A flock of gulls will spread itself out among the lapwings – sometimes, it seems, with individual gulls marking individuals in the other team, like footballers. When a lapwing finds a worm or other edible creature, the gull will fly at it and try to snatch the food, or even twist and turn in the air behind the fleeing lapwing, hoping to make it drop its find.

In summer, when a pair of lapwings is breeding, small birds such as meadow pipits and yellow wagtails will sometimes nest in their territory, knowing that the lapwings will drive off crows or magpies to defend their eggs, and so protect them too. In the winter, the lapwing becomes a victim without a protector.

As September nears its end there is a distinct stirring among the trees again. Birds are getting noisier and more noticeable. In August, so many of them were moulting and hiding quietly among the leaves that you might have thought they had all flown away. A zoologist friend said to me: 'Of course, the reason everybody thinks that the French have killed all their birds is that they go there for their holiday in August.'

One of the first birds to be heard again, piping and exclaiming and whispering as it hunts among the twigs, is the coal tit. It was included, to many people's surprise, on the list of the 12 commonest garden birds published in 1993 by the British Trust for Ornithology. Far fewer people have heard of the coal tit than of its colourful relatives, the blue and great tits.

It is even smaller than the blue tit, and is silvery grey, with a black cap and a very conspicuous white patch on the nape,

It is predominantly a bird of the conifers, which is one reason why it has become commoner in recent years. The spread of pine and fir planatations has given it a boost, so it has increased among the oaks and beeches as well.

Also, it is very good at looking after itself. It is an animated little bird, forever in pursuit of tiny insects in the trees, constantly hanging upside-down or hovering to snap up elusive, tasty morsels. In snowy weather, these talents serve it well – even if a fir branch is creaking under the weight of snow on it, the coal tit can hover happily underneath it, finding its prey as usual.

All the same, the coal tits are adaptable enough to come in considerable numbers to gardens where food is put out, and that is why they got on to the BTO list. They particularly like peanut dispensers, and they have a further trick to help their food supply in the winter: they carry the peanuts off and hide them for another snowy day.

What else is moving and calling in the trees now? The summer visitors have mostly gone, the winter visitors have hardly begun to arrive, and it is our well-adapted resident birds that are making the most of the last insects and the ripe seeds and berries.

Robins and wrens keep their individual territories throughout the winter, and are singing out their challenges to their neighbours as vigorously as they were in the summer. In fact, just now there is quite a riot of song and fighting going on, as the first-year robins and wrens stake their claim to land.

On sunny days in late September and early October, quite a few other birds can be heard singing: chaffinches giving a few trills, great tits with their slow 'see-saw, see-saw' song, and coal tits themselves, whose song sounds rather like a speeded-up version of the great tit's.

Recent studies have shown that even birds that flock

Tawny Owl

together to find food in the winter often keep one foot in their own territory, so to speak. They sing and defend their patch from time to time, so that when spring comes they will have somewhere to start in finding a good place to breed.

The autumn singers which are now piping up are putting in a few ranging shots. Some of the songs you hear are rather scratchy and broken: these come from young birds, who have to practise before they get the music right.

It is the same out on farmland, where the sky suddenly fills with skylark song about now. The British larks will feed together in the winter, skirling across the fields, just like the big flocks of immigrants that are starting to come in across the North Sea. But they will remember their territories, and assert their right to them with scraps of song and brief skirmishes whenever the winter sun is warm enough.

The night is not exempt from this renewed activity. The hooting of the tawny owls that is starting to enliven the darkness is just the one part of the goings-on that we can detect.

Unseen, on their soft and silent wings, the owls are battling hard for the mouse-filled gardens that they would all like best to live in.

Have you seen a bird shaped like a dagger, careering through the sky like a lunatic, and screaming like the devil? If so, you were not having a nightmare; it was a ring-necked parakeet.

These birds from the jungle edges of Africa and Asia have established themselves in many parks and gardens round London, and have also nested around Manchester. They are typical parakeets, with blunt heads and very long tapering tails, and when they are crossing an open space they fly faster and more wildly than any of our native woodland birds.

Their plumage is mainly bright yellow-green, and

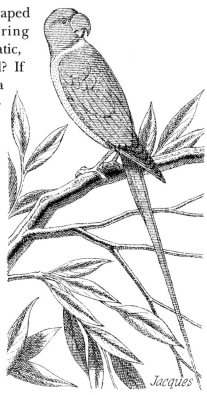

Ring-necked Parakeet

they have a hooked red beak. The male has a ring round its neck, black in front, rose-red on the nape (they are known alternatively as rose-ringed parakeets). The male also has a blue sheen, especially on the head. The female sports a fainter, emerald-coloured neck-ring. They are not always screeching. Sometimes they sit quite quietly in the treetops, preening themselves, and making starling-like whistles and murmurs.

No one knows quite where they came from. Some doubtless escaped from aviaries; others might have been released by sailors who brought them home without realizing they would have to be put into quarantine. They were first recorded breeding in this country in 1969 in Kent, and they have been breeding in Greater London since 1973. In 1983 they were put officially on the British List – in C category, which consists of 'established feral birds that are self-maintaining'.

They certainly maintain themselves all right. They eat any kind of nuts, fruit or human scraps; apples and crab-apples, rose-hips and hawthorn berries, horse-chestnuts and hornbeam seeds. In winter they come to bird-tables, where they dominate all the other birds. However, in Britain they have not yet been seen hunting for fruit in the company of swarms of monkeys, as happens in India.

They seem to be very successful breeders. Paired birds stay together. They take over the old nesting-holes of green and great spotted woodpeckers, or sometimes find a hole under a roof. They lay three or four round white eggs, often as early in the year as January or February, and a good many of their offspring are brought safely to maturity.

Their numbers will probably go on increasing and, if that happens, they could become a menace in fruit-growing areas such as Kent. They do not even finish an apple when they start it. They take a few pecks, then move to another. Their ancestors were used to tropical luxuriance. But I hope they will not be persecuted here. I like their brilliant colours and their frantic life-style – and always look up when I hear that blood-curdling cry overhead.

OCTOBER

Red-necked phalaropes are sometimes recorded along our coasts in early October. These are usually 'gale birds' as the phalaropes are sometimes called in North America – blown here on their way south from their nesting-sites just below the Arctic Circle.

About 20 pairs nest in Great Britain, in the north of Scotland and in the Shetland Islands. I have watched them on the shores of Lake Myvatn, in the north of Iceland. I walked down from my lakeside hotel through a flock of screaming arctic terns that were breeding at the water's edge, and looked out at the great lake, where hundreds of wigeon were up-ending and whooper swans were calling like bellowing cuckoos.

Then suddenly I saw these two tiny birds bobbing about on the water only a few yards from my feet. It was the bird I had come to Iceland above all to look for, and here it was on the doorstep the first day.

They were so tame that I could see all their fine colouring without needing to raise my field-glasses. They have white cheeks, and a scarlet band curling back from their foreheads and down their necks. Their backs are a speckled yellowish-brown and their underparts are white. They are actually waders – close relatives of the plovers and sandpipers. But they are adapted for life on the water, with lobes on the side of their toes, and downy feathers beneath them which trap the air and make them as buoyant as ducks. In fact they sit so lightly on the water that in rough weather they have to take to the land.

I watched my pair feeding, their heads nodding constantly as they picked up midges from the water on all sides. One of them ran ashore after an insect, then ran back into the lake again. Then the other suddenly began the display for which they are famous – spinning round and round on the water to stir up the mosquito larvae.

There is something else for which phalaropes are famous – the male does all the incubation and brings up the family entirely by himself. The female is the more brightly coloured of the pair. She does the wooing, chooses the nest-site – a scrape or a tussock on the shore – and lays the eggs, then she calls it a day. If there are spare males around, she will sometimes mate with another one, and leave him to the same fate too. There are generally four young, and they keep close to their father like young ducklings for a fortnight after they have fledged. In fact it is said:

The phalarope, although red-necked,
Is also dreadfully henpecked.

The arctic terns who dived at my head every time I watched the phalaropes are not unconnected with their lives. The phalaropes often nest deliberately near a colony of terns, who provide a protective shield above them. But the breeding season is short in those high latitudes, and soon after nesting they are on their way south to warmer coasts.

By October they have generally lost their summer plumage. The birds that turn up in England in autumn are hard to distinguish from another phalarope – the grey phalarope, which breeds even further north by the ephemeral pools of the high tundra. Both these species are now grey and white, with the grey phalarope a little lighter in tone. It is worth making the visit to Iceland just to watch the red-necked phalaropes spinning on the water in their full summer brilliance.

The starling is the bird that once stopped the chimes of Big Ben. So many of them perched on the minute hand one evening that the clock could not strike nine. But these were only a handful out of the great flocks that come to roost in London on winter nights.

It is in October that city people become most aware of them. This is the time of the year when the birds arrive overhead just as humans are coming out into the streets on their way home. The birds come sweeping in and settle on roofs and pinnacles and, above all, the ledges of tall office

Starling

buildings. Instantly, they start singing – wheezing and chattering and croaking in a chorus that sounds like an aeroplane engine starting up. They often rise in a black wave into the sky again, and twist and manoeuvre in the air before finally settling.

Enormous numbers of starlings migrate to Britain in October from the Continent, some from as far as Poland or Russia (although numbers have fallen in the past few years). It was once thought that the roosting birds in our towns were these immigrants. Now it is known that most are from the suburbs.

The starlings that have been feeding in gardens and playing fields gather in local rendezvous in trees in the late afternoon, then fly together into the town centre, picking up others as they pass. I once saw a starling on a chimney pot near Baker Street in London, singing its territorial song and flapping its wings in defiance as a huge horde of other starlings flew overhead. It was persisting with its daytime behaviour, defending its nest-hole against possible invaders. Doubtless a few minutes later it flew up to join them in Trafalgar Square.

Many of the birds come back to the same spot on a ledge every evening. There they shuffle about and quarrel and chatter all night. On very cold nights they huddle wing to wing. They cannot get much unbroken sleep, but they feel safe. They began this roosting in London on a large scale at about the beginning of the First World War, and they have also invaded many other towns. They whitewash every building they sleep on, and attempts are always being made to get rid of them. Some years ago, in Belgium, an immense flock started roosting in some cherry orchards. They were blasted out with dynamite and three-quarters of a million birds were killed. Within a few years, their numbers had completely recovered.

Starlings also form big roosts in the country, in woods and copses, especially among prickly blackthorn and hawthorn. Here the woodland floor is devastated by their droppings. In the country, you can see spectacular sights before they settle down. The flocks unite and part and meet again in the sky, sometimes catching up a passing woodpigeon in their aerial dives, leaving it bewildered. From a distance, they look like swirling plumes of smoke.

In the morning, starlings do not leave their roosts with one ear-cracking roar of wings, but set out in groups, flying in all directions, at about three-minute intervals.

They go back to their own localities, forage, keep an eye on their nest-holes, sing in a desultory way. They may descend on a garden or field and leave the grass full of holes where they have been digging for insects. Now you can see that their plumage is not just black, but spangled with lighter dots, with a glossy green or purple sheen when they catch the light.

They are energetic and successful scavengers, and often have time to spare, sitting in idle groups on a bare branch. But as the winter sun sinks, they are off again – for another long night on the tiles.

There are few sights more cheering than a little flock of jackdaws stalking briskly around some sheep, their eyes gleaming and the autumn sunshine bringing out the soft grey of their caps. They are such lively birds, pouncing on a beetle here, leaping up to catch a dung-fly there, forever on the move.

They are quite unlike the rooks they sometimes mix with. While the jackdaws pick up all their food from the grass, the rooks dig steadily into the ground for worms and leatherjackets, and their progress across a field is far more stately.

When they are startled and all fly up from the field, the two species also behave quite differently. You get a few protesting caws from the rooks, but the jackdaws fire off a positive salvo of indignant clackings, and the whole sky seems in uproar for a moment.

There are probably about three million jackdaws in Britain at the beginning of October, including this year's surviving youngsters. But during the next few weeks their numbers will be swollen by winter migrants from Scandinavia.

They roost at night in woods, often with rooks and crows, though the jackdaws usually stay in a separate clump of trees. Before they go to bed they give spectacular flying displays, tumbling out of the sky like volcanic debris, then righting themselves and wheeling and shooting up again, with a cannonade of wild clacking.

They fly all day around the cathedral roofs in Paris and Florence – but not around London's St Paul's. The fields are too far away.

The place to go to look for birds in mid-October is a dug-up potato field. I came across one last week that was crowded with them. There is not much to glean on the corn stubble these days, but a turned-up potato field offers an abundance of exposed seeds and insects.

A cloud of birds went up as I climbed the gate. They were not hard to identify as linnets. The sun caught their chestnut backs, and their twanging calls reached me clearly in the still air.

Several pied wagtails were running about on the earth among the potato sacks, bouncing up and down as they skirmished with each other. But the persistent skirmishers were the skylarks.

The horizon was full of them, making their liquid calls and chasing each other. Most of them were doubtless young males beginning to assert themselves. Two skylarks – probably older, settled males – were singing tirelessly overhead. The hedge at the far end of the field was also busy. It was crimson and blue with hawthorn berries and sloes, but the birds in it were not interested. They were waiting to go down to the field. Several yellowhammers were skulking behind the hedge, and suddenly, on the top of one bush, I saw a tree sparrow.

It was easily distinguished from a house sparrow, with its black cheek patches and chestnut cap. It had four or five companions in the hedge. These dapper little birds have become uncommon – and I stood watching them until they got bored and flew away.

As the leaves begin to fall, the winter movements of the bird population begin to make themselves felt. Jays that have nested in the woods start appearing in town gardens. They are still shy, and most often come at dawn, before many people are stirring. They hop heavily along a garage roof, looking for edible scraps – running spiders or fallen seeds in the gutter.

They seem too beautiful to belong to the crow family, with their pink plumage and the streak of electric blue in their wings. But their voices are raucous enough for a crow, and one often hears a visiting jay's loud screeches before one sees it. Then a stout bird slips over a wall with hesitant beats of its rounded wings, and you see a last flash of its white rump as it vanishes into another garden.

Jay

Jays often lead the angry chorus if a tawny owl ventures out of the ivy in the daytime. They scream and fly at it, and blackbirds, thrushes and chaffinches join in, without approaching the owl too closely. They usually succeed in driving the owl away.

Jays also have an autumn song, which I have heard once or twice, though it is rather rare and its function is quite obscure. The singer sits in the depths of a holly tree or other dense bush and produces a long string of creaking, carolling notes in a low voice.

Great spotted woodpeckers are often very conspicuous at this time of the year; they sit on the very tip of a fir tree, and are not easily disturbed. They are black and white birds with a bright red patch on the underside between the stomach and the tail; the male also has a red nape and the juveniles have a red crown.

This is another bird that is frequently heard before it is seen. It makes a distinctive resounding 'chack' call – always a single note. They wedge nuts in a hole in a bough before cracking them open with their beaks. Nowadays they come down and take nuts from bird tables; they can even hammer open almond stones without damage to their specially padded brains. They also have a long tongue with which to lick up insects.

With most of the summer visitors gone and winter visitors from the Continent only just starting to arrive, there are far fewer small birds about, and sparrow-hawks begin to range more widely now in search of prey. They have various techniques: sometimes they will circle high in the sky looking for movement in the trees below, then come down and hide before sweeping out through the branches and picking up a goldcrest or long-tailed tit. At other times they go hedge-hopping, speeding down one side and swinging over to take a robin by surprise.

However, these small birds have their own technique for puzzling a sparrow-hawk. All of them have thin, ventriloquial alarm notes that make them hard to locate – perhaps even harder for a bird-watcher than for a raptor. Sparrow-hawks, by the way, are steadily getting commoner in towns.

The winter visitors will make the next change in the character of the countryside – the winter thrushes and finches coming in mainly from northern Europe. They will form much of the tale in the weeks ahead.

The fieldfares are arriving. A loud 'chack-chack-chack', like a crackle of machine-gun fire, rings out somewhere in the sky. Then two or three of them sweep by – big thrushes, flying rather erratically, with a few powerful wing beats repeatedly followed by a brief glide. Suddenly they are all round you – flying up from the field, flying out of the trees, most of them calling. Winter has announced its return.

About a million of them come down to Britain every year at this time from their breeding grounds anywhere between Stockholm and the Arctic Circle. When the autumn's crop of bright red rowan berries has been eaten up, they gather in flocks and head south-west.

They are about the size of mistle-thrushes but much more dramatically coloured; you cannot mistake the powder-blue head, the chestnut back, the blue-grey rump and the black tail. On the breast they are golden-brown streaked with black, and under the tail they are white. They look as much like banners as birds.

Here in Britain they flock into the hawthorn trees for berries. They also feed out in the fields, and when the weather gets hard they will come into gardens. Fallen apples still lying on the grass are much sought after at the end of the year.

They may be colourful birds, but they have a feeble song compared with most thrushes. It is a rather thin, tuneless string of warbling notes. This lack of vigour is probably because they nest colonially and do not defend their territories in the way that other thrushes do.

Across Scandinavia and much of northern Europe the fieldfares' song has long been a familiar summer sound, but in this century it has been heard much more frequently further south, in Belgium and Switzerland, for instance. In Great Britain, the first pair was discovered in 1967, and since then there have generally been a few pairs recorded breeding here, most of them in Scotland and the Pennines.

However, they also have a babbling winter song – a kind of

mixture of their summer notes and their winter calls. Just as the crackle in the sky portends winter, this cheerful chorus always evokes the coming of spring again for me.

The first beechnuts are falling. The hard, hairy nutshells split open to reveal a pair of triangular seeds, which all too often are like little withered commas, with nothing inside except dark brown fur. But in a good year you find many with sweet, plump white flesh under the brown rind.

A good year for beech mast can also be a good one for bramblings. These are finches from Scandinavia and Finland that mostly eat beechnuts in winter. They are often found with chaffinches, to which they are closely related. They are the only two species of British finch that can run or walk on the ground – the others hop.

At first glance, bramblings might be mistaken for chaffinches, but they are more orange than pink on the breast, and also have orange shoulders and a darker head. When they fly up they are easily distinguished by their conspicuous white rump.

Bramblings are among the most opportunistic of migrants, having no regular winter quarters but going each year where the beech mast is most abundant. Some years they are quite common in Britain.

The most astonishing winter that has been recorded in their history was 1946–47. That year there was a great beech harvest in Switzerland and vast flocks of them descended on the country. There may have been as many as 100 million – practically the whole breeding population of northern Europe.

In Britain, most winters, I feel lucky to get a glimpse of a single one! But good beechnut years hold out the promise of better things.

Tufted Duck

Riding out on the water on the many lakes and ponds now is a little black-and-white duck. The patch of white plumage abuts the water along the duck's flanks; sometimes the bird rolls over and shows it has a whole gleaming white under-side. If you get closer, you can see it has a short black pigtail and bright yellow eyes.

This is the drake tufted duck – 'drake duck' sounds odd, but phrases like 'tufted drake' have also come to sound pedantic. I also have to call the other sex 'the female', because 'the duck' would be ambiguous and 'the duck duck' would sound absurd. Anyway, she is dark brown, but is likewise paler on the flanks, and she too sports the pigtail or tuft.

This is another species that has become a common breeding bird in Britain only in comparatively recent times –

it was first recorded in 1824. In the present century, it has benefited greatly from the increase in gravel pits with overgrown banks on which it can nest.

They are more widespread from October onward because many come here to winter from northern Scandinavia and Siberia. Some of our native birds will mate with these immigrants and go back home with them – a practice known as abmigration.

When they are in active mood they are a delight to watch. They are diving ducks, picking up molluscs or weed seeds from the bottom of a lake, and they will go down as many as a hundred times an hour. Generally they dive with a slight leap forward. They stay down for about 20 seconds, and you never know where they are going to bob up again. Sometimes they are found in large flocks, all going up and down.

In early spring, one of the most delightful sounds to be heard from a lakeside comes from little groups of tufted ducks, as the drakes start courting. They make a soft, bell-like note, only audible for a short distance. The sunshine brings out a brilliant purple gloss on their heads, which they throw back excitedly as part of their courting display, letting their tufts dangle. Sometimes you hear a growling note from the female.

They have paired up by April, but they are slow to nest after that. It will be almost June before they start building under a bush or in thick grass. Once started, however, they are energetic, with the female commonly laying a dozen large eggs or more. The brown ducklings are out on the water as soon as they hatch and are diving within a few hours.

Many of them will fall victim to pike and heron. But some will still be there to join the winter flocks when they come down from the north – and perhaps, when the spring days lengthen, will be off to breed with a foreign mate.

How do you tell a rook from a crow? People have not always been able to make the distinction. Scarecrows, for example, should really be called 'scarerooks', because that is what they mainly do, or try to do.

However, the rook and the crow are quite different species, though they are both black birds of the fields. Rooks can best be distinguished by the bare white patch on their face at the base of the bill, and by their rather shaggy thighs when they plod about on the ground. Crows have wholly black, well-feathered faces, and trim legs.

When one of them sweeps past you, it is more difficult. I always think of the rook as the more elegant-looking bird. It flaps its wings slightly quicker, but more nonchalantly, with the tips of the feathers often spread in a rather languid way. Crows – or carrion crows, to give them their full name – have a more deliberate, sinister wing beat, and forge on across the sky determinedly. Also, the crow's caw is deeper and more resonant, the rook's varied and yelping. But you cannot entirely trust such impressions.

A further difference is that rooks stay mostly in flocks and, of course, breed in rookeries, with many nests in adjoining treetops. The crow is generally thought of as a solitary bird, but when you see one it is rarely more than few seconds before you see its mate coming over the horizon. It is the pairs rather than the individuals which are solitary.

I like both rooks and crows. I especially like the sight of a flock of rooks rising from a ploughed field with the sun catching their glossy backs and turning them all to silver. But I always feel a deep contentment – a sense that nature can be trusted – when I see that second crow appear.

Young carrion crows are more sociable. They roam together in the autumn and the old crows try to keep them out of their territories. You hear the rattling cry of an angry crow quite often just now, as the generations clash.

Crows also sometimes join rooks and jackdaws in their woodland roosts. Some commentators have said that Shakespeare got the species mixed up when he wrote in *Macbeth* that at sunset 'the crow makes wing to the rooky wood'. But he was right. Shakespeare the countryman seems to have been a bit of a bird-watcher.

NOVEMBER

A low piping note in the bushes tells you that a bullfinch is there. But it is a shy bird and you may get only a glimpse of a white rump flitting through the branches. That is true even in spring.

A charming poem by Thomas Hardy begins 'Brother bullies, let us sing' – but this is misleading, because bullfinches are the only small English birds that scarcely sing at all.

They do not normally defend a territory in the breeding season – they just get on with nesting – so there is no need in spring for the male to perch on a conspicuous twig, as a chaffinch does, and sing its heart out to warn off other males.

The male bullfinch is a fine sight. His breast is a deeper pink than the chaffinch's; his back is a soft grey and he has a black cap that tilts just over his beak.

The female has the black cap but is otherwise a brownish-grey. She is usually nearby and the pair pipe frequently to each other to keep in touch.

In autumn they feed on birch catkins and dried-up blackberries; as winter comes they turn to the brown seeds dangling on the bare branches of the ash trees.

But these food supplies often run out by the New Year and they then start eating buds on fruit trees. Pears, plums, cherries and gooseberries are all attacked. They eat the small embryonic centre of each bud, the part that would otherwise turn to fruit, and drop the rest.

This means that the birds are hated by orchard owners, and in counties such as Kent and Essex commercial fruit-growers can get a licence to trap and kill them between 1 November and 30 April. (Ordinary gardeners find it more difficult to get permission.) The usual practice is to trap the birds at the beginning of winter in the hope that with fewer birds around the natural food will last until spring.

However, the bullfinches suffer from this less than might be thought. According to the Ministry of Agriculture only 326 of them were taken in one recent year – and some of these may not have been killed, because the fruit-growers are allowed to sell them or give them away for breeding in captivity.

They are also well prepared for the winter, as their plumage at this time of the year is heavier than in summer. This means that their feathers altogether weigh one-and-a-half grams now, compared with one gram before the moult – but that half-gram makes all the difference to them. It is easy to forget how light most birds are.

The first thing I saw when I got to the lake the other day was a female reed-bunting feeding vigorously on the purple seed-heads of the phragmites reeds. She was swaying with the tops of the reeds, and was so absorbed that she let me have a good view of the beautiful, finely inked striations on her back, and of her rather unfeminine moustache.

Out beyond the reeds, coots were making pinging cries, and tufted ducks were diving, while a pair of mute swans were quietly preening. When they had finished, each gave a brisk, self-satisfied wag of its pointed white tail.

But the most dramatic birds on the lake were a party of eight cormorants. Seven of them were sitting on a raft, their beaks pointing up in that suspicious way they have, and two of them had spread their wings out to dry.

One had its wings in a W-shape, and was gently flapping the tips of them. The other had them stretched out straight, like the hem of a large black curtain. The eighth bird was swimming very low in the water, and suddenly dived. They chase eels under-water, using their feet as propellers – but this one came up with nothing.

Anglers and fish farmers hate cormorants as much as many country folk hate magpies. They can get a licence to shoot them if serious damage to fish stocks is proved. But the RSPB points out that there are only about 7,500 pairs of them in Britain – so I am glad to learn that licences are quite hard to get.

There was a report in the journal *British Birds* not long ago of the strange death of a goldcrest in Cumbria. This tiny bird, with its brilliant orange crown, had been trapped in a burdock plant by the hooked seeds. These are the brown seeds that cling to your clothes if you brush against them at this time of the year. The goldcrest had not been able to escape from their clutches, and had died there.

It was unlucky inasmuch as it had wandered away from its usual haunts, which are the branches of conifer trees. Sometimes a pair of goldcrests will take up residence in a solitary cedar or a great silver fir in a garden and, as Lord Grey of Fallodon put it years ago in his book *The Charm of Birds*, 'each tree becomes a whole world to them'.

Grey has a good description of the goldcrest's song, which can be heard in the conifers, even in winter on sunny days:

'Like a tiny stream trickling and rippling over a small pebbly channel, and at the end going over a miniature cascade.'

However, the correspondent in the journal also reported that he had found two goldcrests caught in spiders' webs in the same area, so perhaps the goldcrests in that part of Cumbria are particularly accident-prone.

In addition, there was a report of a swallow in Germany that had been caught by its wings in a burdock, which is even more surprising. The goldcrest might have been looking for insects, but the swallow must simply have hit the plant when flying low. It was suggested that the swallow, with its weak feet, could not lever itself out. Yet a flock of greenfinches nearby were perching on the seed heads and extricating the seeds without any difficulty.

However, the swallow was luckier than the goldcrest. The

Goldcrest

people who found it took it out and cleaned it up, and it swept away to join other swallows feeding over the Rhine.

Incidentally, if you look this report up in *British Birds*, you will find that it is about a 'barn swallow'. Do not be puzzled. This is the new, official ornithological name for our common European swallow. *British Birds* has been discreet in adopting new names, but this one it has accepted. The problem is, that with ornithology becoming so international, an extra description seemed necessary to distinguish our swallow clearly from all the other swallows in the world.

Birds can get caught in other ways. There is a record of a song-thrush being entangled in thorns on a blackberry bush, where it was eaten by a cat. A more bizarre fate befell a garden blackbird, which got its wings caught in the network of symmetrically arranged twigs in a mock orange tree.

The feral pigeons in London have another problem. Wandering about as they do on pavements and in gutters, they have a tendency to get bits of thread and cotton twined round their legs, which get tied together. This chafes their legs and makes it hard for them to walk, and sometimes they will even lose a leg.

The writer Naomi Lewis goes round London with a small pair of scissors especially to help them. She has become expert at spotting pigeons in this plight, pouncing on them, picking them up, and cutting them free.

Many of the pigeons in Trafalgar Square and other parts of London are almost indistinguishable from the rock doves of the Scottish sea cliffs, and are descendants of rock doves, who had a different kind of escape early in this century.

Rock doves were brought down in baskets by train from Scotland and used as sporting targets at the Hurlingham Club in south-west London. They were released from boxes with collapsible sides and shot at from 25 yards range. They were liked for the sport because they were so quick and lively on the wing, and many got away; but they stayed on in London. The practice came to an end only in 1910 with the passing of the Captive Animals Act.

There used to be a story going round in shooting circles of one bird that rescued itself in its troubles. This was the story of a woodcock which was supposed to have broken its leg, and bandaged it by its own efforts. It was said to have been found with blades of grass and narrow rushes neatly wrapped round the fracture, and the whole thing set in a plaster of mud.

It is possible that someone out shooting found such a bird. But I am afraid that, if so, the woodcock had just dragged its wounded leg along behind it and picked up grass and mud which had hardened on to it.

Birds can be very resourceful at times. But the woodcock which gave itself first aid must be retired, I fancy, to the realm of myth.

Great auks are extinct, but the little auk lives on. It is a very little auk indeed, about 8in tall when standing on a clifftop, and it lives mainly within the Arctic Circle. It has a stubby beak that gives it a face like a frog, and it nests in rock fissures that have been cracked open by the frost.

The birds feed on plankton around the pack ice, and even in winter only a few come very far south.

In the first half of November, however, small flocks of little auks do pass along the east coast of Britain, though well out to sea. They are seen by the hardened coastal watchers, who will stand all day looking out to sea, armed with powerful telescopes.

As the little auks speed over the waves, they look more like starlings than seabirds, and they soon pass out of sight.

It is only when there are fierce storm winds at sea that they are found inland in this country, and then they are usually dead. In February 1983, about 1,200 corpses of little auks were found on the east side of England.

However, in the high Arctic they are thriving. They wheel in flocks round their breeding sites like swarms of insects.

The great auks of Greenland and Newfoundland died out in 1844, the victims of fishermen who ate them and their eggs, until there were none left. But there may still be as many as 30 million little auks in the world. Some ornithologists think that little auks are the most abundant seabird. So their chances look a little brighter than those of their great cousins.

Leaves are drifting along the rivers of Britain, and the reeds are beginning to sink by their banks. But there is plenty of life out on the water. Coots call with an ear-piercing note, like someone taking an angry blow at a metal sheet with a sharp hammer. Coots are, in fact, rather angry birds, sometimes fighting to the death in spring, and even now sailing menacingly towards each other, with necks low on the water, when they feel offended. However, they are brave, too: I once saw a ferocious-looking arctic skua that had wandered far from its oceanic home come down on a lake in Hertfordshire, and immediately a coot swam up and pecked it.

Normally, they float about in a rather sulky way, all black apart from the white shield above their beak, which reflects brightly in still water. They rarely come ashore, unlike their relatives the moorhens.

On the water, moorhens tend to stay under overhanging branches. Their heads jerk to and fro as they swim along, and there is a good reason for this. It means that they can keep their eyes steadily on a stretch of water as they move forward, and scrutinize it thoroughly for food. Their heads are not so much nodding as catching up with their bodies.

Moorhens often scramble up the bank on to the towpath, and there they flick their tails as well, revealing a large crescent of white beneath. Now you can also see their long green legs, with which they step in a dandy-like way over the grass. Sometimes a large number will gather in a field – but at the slightest alarm the whole flock flees back to the water, tails up, necks thrust forward, sometimes with a desperate flutter of wings that lifts them briefly off the ground.

Mallards also lurk along the bank, and an occasional tufted duck can be seen diving out in the middle, but most ducks are more lake birds than river birds. You are just as likely to see a great crested grebe, half asleep, its head tucked into its silky feathers.

Herons feed along lonely banks; you need to look far ahead along the river to see one standing in the shallows, since they will not let you get close. They lumber up on heavy wings, M-shaped against the sky as you watch them beat away.

If you are lucky, as you continue along the towpath you will hear another piercing call, a shade more vibrant and mellow than the coot's. It is a kingfisher, and it passes you like a blob of blue light. It might stop not much farther on and perch on the open bank of the river, where it reveals itself as perhaps the most exotic of all British birds; turquoise back, white throat, orange under-parts.

You might think that such a bird could never camouflage itself – but I have detected them in autumn sitting in a waterside bramble bush, where they are almost indiscernible among the green and scarlet leaves. They dive for fish, not always successfully, and come back to the branch they have

Kingfisher

been sitting on in a shower of waterdrops.

There are always, of course, plenty of small birds in the riverside hedges – wrens chattering, chaffinches looping away with a soft twitter, blackbirds and thrushes. Two small birds more particularly of the water's edge are the grey wagtail and, occasionally, the meadow pipit.

Grey wagtails have a grey back and a spectacular yellow breast; they also have the longest and most energetic tails of all the wagtails. They are brisk and curious searchers for insects; at this time of year I have seen them walking on fallen leaves floating in a ditch.

Water-rail

The thin piping of the meadow pipit is a moorland sound in the summer, but you can sometimes hear it now in riverside meadows, as winter immigrants fly up and disappear on typically weak-looking wing beats.

The really elusive bird of the riverside is another rail, like the coots and moorhens: the water-rail. Water-rails are not uncommon in winter, but they mostly slip unseen through reeds and the thick tangle of the bank. Just occasionally they will come boldly out and stalk along in full view. Then you can see their beautifully streaked upper parts, their pink legs and long red beak. A moment later they blend with the vegetation and are gone. Dusk is the best time for seeing them, and it is also when they are noisiest, squeaking and squealing in the depths of their retreats. To see or just hear one makes a dramatic end to a winter's day by the river.

The goldcrest is the smallest British bird, measuring less than 4in long and weighing only six grams, but its tiny brain allows it to perform wonderful acrobatic feats.

I was watching one feeding last week in a newly naked sycamore tree. It darted, it hovered and finally it hung upside-down, which is what I wanted it to do, because until then I had not clearly seen the golden-orange stripe along the top of the bird's head. Now, for a moment, I could see the stripe sparkling, even though the day was misty.

The goldcrest has ridges on the underside of its minuscule toes which allow it to get a good grip and even to cling on to a pine needle. It has a very fine bill, which is also relatively long, to tease out minute insects from the twigs. It is commonest in pine and fir woods – it is one of the few species to have flourished with the increased planting of conifers – but it quite often moves into deciduous trees in winter.

Goldcrests like to travel around with the flocks of titmice at this time of year, and they are very similar to coal tits in their feeding habits, but nowadays they are classed along with the chiffchaff and willow warbler among the sub-family of Old World warblers. They are not shy, once you have found them, but they are quite difficult to locate by ear. They are good ventriloquists, and their thin calls seem to come now from one side of a fir tree, now the other. It all helps to confuse passing sparrow-hawks.

When I first saw the little green bird last week I was particularly anxious to get a good view, because in recent years two rare warblers that look rather like it have been recorded in a number of places – the yellow-browed warbler and Pallas's warbler. Both species have creamy eyestripes but no crest; Pallas's warbler also has a yellow rump.

My bird proved to be one of the two or three million goldcrests that are found in Britain early in the winter. But it is worth having a good look at any one that you find – just in case it is a Siberian rarity.

Millions of ducks and geese head south and west through Europe in November, many of them destined for Britain. They fly high, at night, and are more often heard than seen, as they call to each other. But in the morning, there they are, drifting on a lake or on the ebbing waters of an estuary.

Among the most spectacular are the wigeon, which come from Scandinavia or even as far as Siberia. In Britain, a few pairs nest around the Scottish lochs, but in winter there can be up to 40,000 of them on the Ouse Washes or on the mudflats at Lindisfarne.

They are noisy ducks, constantly whistling – a sudden, sharp whistle, that really rings out on a frosty morning. The drakes have chestnut heads with a buttery patch above the beak, and silvery body-plumage. Both sexes have white sterns, and when a large flock is all 'up-ending' out on the water, they look like a flotilla of miniature sailing-boats.

They are opportunistic feeders, and when swans put their long necks under water and draw up weeds from the bottom, the wigeon will gather round and pick up other fragments loosened by the swans. They have even been seen pulling a blade of eelgrass from a swan's beak.

A still more beautiful duck with a strange way of feeding is the shoveler. It is a bird of inland lakes rather than estuaries, and the highest numbers are generally found in November, so this is a good moment to look for them.

The drakes have a green head, a shining white breast, orange flanks and a streak of white in front of the tail. They seem more like a national flag than a bird. They also have an extraordinary beak, from which they get their name – a long, rectangular spatula.

The shoveler lays its beak flat on the water, or just under it, and steams forward. Its tongue moves up and down, sucking the water in from the front, and pumping it out through the side of the beak, which is lined with tiny teeth. The teeth filter out and trap the tiny food particles in the water that the bird wants.

Two exotic ducks that have naturalized themselves here also turn up more widely on lakes and ponds in the winter, and are well worth looking out for – the mandarin and the ruddy duck.

The mandarin is an oriental bird and the drake might almost be mistaken for a geisha girl. He has a red beak, and flowing white feathers on the top of his orange head; on his wings he has big orange sleeves. The female has silvery, marbled plumage. They like swimming in the shadows under overhanging rhododendron bushes, and in the autumn they feed on the woodland floor, looking for acorns and chestnuts. Their headquarters in Britain is Windsor Great Park, where they find just the conditions they like round Virginia Water lake.

The ruddy duck is an American bird with a bright blue beak, a white face and a cocked tail. It has been in trouble in Spain recently for interbreeding with the native white-headed duck there, and threatening the purity of the species.

DECEMBER

Down on the estuary, where the waves cream gently over the sand, there are often many waders stalking about or running in and out of the water. Curlews bow forward to probe with their long, curved beaks; dunlins patter to and fro; ringed plovers stamp on the sand, hoping some succulent little creature will be lured out.

But farther along, where the pebbles and rocks begin, there is not so much life to be seen. Then you suddenly hear a sharp clatter, and you see a turnstone tossing pebbles over to see what is beneath them.

The turnstone, like the wagtail, gets its name from what it does. It spends its life looking under things. Not only does it insert its beak under stones and throw them up with a jerk of its head; it also parts the seaweed fronds, and lifts the sprawling leaves of eelgrass. Sometimes you may see two of them trying to lift a dead fish. What they are always looking for is shrimps, winkles and barnacles.

They are winter visitors to Britain, some coming from Canada and Greenland, some from the high Arctic above Scandinavia. They are quite common on all our shores and are usually found in small parties. In their breeding plumage they have vivid tortoiseshell backs, but by mid-winter much of the colour has gone from them. Even so, they are attractive birds.

They sometimes run fast in pursuit of sandhoppers and

tiny crabs; in flight, they have a boldly pied look that is distinctive among the shore birds. When the waves crash violently over the rocks, they will move inland, feeding among rabbit burrows or in the gutters of seaside houses.

A few non-breeders stay here for the summer, but most go back to the Arctic islands, where they nest on the stones or under low plants. They lay their four speckled eggs in the shape of a cross.

Another winter visitor that can be found with them among the rock pools is an even more northern bird – the purple sandpiper. Many of these stay boldly within the Arctic Circle or in Iceland throughout the winter. They are typical sandpipers, slim and lively, with a down-curved beak. They are very dark birds, but as spring nears their plumage begins to glow with a purple sheen.

Purple sandpipers are remarkably tame, especially when compared with other waders like the nervous, screaming redshanks. They will run behind a retreating wave to pick up a winkle that is tumbling about in the water, then run quickly back again before the next wave breaks.

Like the turnstones, most of them have left Britain by May, and return in the autumn. Now is the time to go down among the sea spray and look for them.

Old flooded gravel pits are where bird-watchers should be as winter closes in. The alder trees along the shores are bursting with life. The alders themselves look quite different from the bare trees around them: their branches are thick with this year's knobbly seed cones and next year's purple catkins.

All seems quiet; then suddenly, the sky is full of small birds that fall into the alder crowns with faint, sweet calls. A flock of siskins has arrived. In no time they are hanging upside-down under the cones, working away at them with their tough little bills.

They are agile and dainty green birds with two distinct yellow wing bars. Their forked tails are very noticeable as they cling to the dark twigs. With the sun on them, the males can be picked out by their black caps and black bibs. They have all probably come south from Scotland, where they nest in the conifer forests.

Something startles them, and the whole flock goes up with a twanging murmur like a rush of air through finely tuned strings. Then they sweep around, and are back in the boughs again.

But one bird looks different. It has a gold wing bar, and its head is red and white. There are goldfinches in the flock, too, a little larger than the siskins but almost as acrobatic. Mixed in the flock one may also find lesser redpolls, much the same size as the siskins and feeding on the alder cones in the same way, but brown with a red cap. The redpolls tend to separate from the other birds in the air and fly off with a hard, rattling call, unmistakable once heard.

Out on the water in the pit there is also plenty of life. Most noticeable will probably be the cormorants. In recent years they have started coming inland more and more in winter. In the London docklands they stand on the top of cranes and look down at the river. In the country they perch on dead trees at the edge of lakes.

They are large birds with snake-like necks and long beaks with a hook at the end. Often they open their wings to dry them. The wind rocks them when they are poised like this. Then they dive again, particularly pursuing eels, or they float in the water with only head and green eye showing.

On every part of the water, coots plod about in an independent-minded way. A shoveler drifts off cautiously when it notices humans. There is perhaps a little grebe diving among a stretch of water plants; whenever it comes up, it is in an unexpected place, and hardly stays long enough to show its crimson neck (fading as winter comes on) and its curiously fluffy rear.

Black-headed gulls are going up and down, screaming all the time. One or two lesser black-backed gulls brood on the far shore, not far from a snipe that is sleeping there with its long beak tucked under its feathers. The markings on its back are among the most beautiful of all British birds: the chestnut feathers are flecked with yellow, and crossed by long, creamy stripes.

As the short day goes by, the scene changes. By mid-afternoon, the gulls are starting to leave for their roosts, winging lightly away in small groups. Some of the cormorants may be off to a bridge across a river, where they will feel safe from marauding foxes. Duck are starting their flight to other pools. But the snipe is probing again in the mud, and small birds are coming in. Pied wagtails are dropping into the reed-beds, linnets into dense bushes.

In the dusk, a late gull cries, some wigeon that have just landed whistle softly. The only avian sound as darkness takes over is the 'chink, chink, chink' of the roosting blackbirds, restless to the last.

The air was chill, the sky was grey, and snow lingered among the dead leaves on the ground. But there was a winter flurry of birds in the trees around me. A robin was bobbing up and down excitedly on a twig, making angry ticking sounds – and I could hear the rival robin that it was getting excited about making similar calls further over in the undergrowth.

Just by me, there were eight or nine blackbirds in a dense hawthorn tree that was still loaded with darkening red berries. The twigs and berries were so thick that you could not see the blackbirds in the middle of them, but some of them kept flying out in alarm, then surreptitiously making their way back. Others emerged to eat a berry on an outer twig. They held it for a moment in the middle of their open beak, silhouetted against the sky, before swallowing it, then plunged back into the tree for more.

A moment later, the branches around were full of small, dancing shapes. A restless flock of titmice had arrived. Long-tailed tits fell with a twist of their body from a high to a lower branch, as if they were tiny, spent rockets. They hung on a twig for a moment, furiously pecking at a bud with an insect in it, then dropped off and looped away to another tree.

Great tits were shooting like puffs of blue smoke from tree to tree, always pausing to look to left and right when they landed, and giving one a chance to see their yellow breasts divided by a bold black streak. Blue tits seemed to linger longer on a spray when they found something to interest their stomachs. All the tits were calling – the long-tailed tits muttering to themselves, the blue tits making brief trills, the great tits making sharper, more ringing notes.

Then, suddenly, somewhere among them, I heard a chiffchaff. Chiffchaffs have a liquid 'hweet' call, a common sound in our woods in the summer, and that was what I was hearing. But try as I might, I could not pick it out among all these small silhouettes of birds, flickering among the last damp leaves that dotted the branches.

Most chiffchaffs have gone to the Mediterranean by December, but in recent years a few have always wintered in the south of England. No one is sure whether these are birds that nested here, or birds from further north that came in on the autumn migration and decided to stay.

I would have liked to see it and confirm that I had correctly identified its call. But by now the whole flock was tripping away to another part of the woods. These mixed winter flocks go round and round a stretch of woodland, picking up all the obvious insects, and not wasting time hunting for the hidden ones.

So I too went on my way, and saw a few ducks and coots that I had seen the day before, and got a glimpse of a heron, its head sunk in its shoulders, by a distant ditch. It was getting towards dusk, and I disturbed a pheasant that had gone to roost in a tree, as I made my way home.

Then, suddenly, I heard the 'hweet' call again. This time it was coming from a hedge at the edge of the wood. A bird was slipping through the twigs, and it paused long enough for me to get my glasses on it.

I could not see its greeny-buff colour in the half-light – but in combination with its note, its slim, graceful form was unmistakable. I had seen my wintering chiffchaff after all.

Out in the middle of the lake, all the waterfowl were black and white. Tufted ducks were leaping forward and disappearing beneath the surface, coots were chugging solemnly along, and a juvenile great crested grebe glided past like a snake that had been twisted into the form of a bird.

But by the bank on the far side there was colour. Some shovelers were pushing their spatula-like beaks through the water, and the bottle-green heads and red flanks of the drakes glowed in the low sun. Then my field-glasses caught sight of another duck. This one had a chestnut-coloured head, with a thin white line down the back of it that might have been painted with a fine brush. The line joined up with the bird's white breast; it had a dappled grey body, and a cream-coloured patch in front of its exquisite, long tail.

I had found a drake pintail – a visitor from its summer breeding ground in northern Europe or western Siberia. Pintails are arriving in large numbers just now, and are mostly gathering along the east coast, or on the estuaries of the Mersey and the Dee. But throughout the winter, odd individuals like mine will turn up at shallow lakes and gravel pits inland.

It swam a little way out from the bank, then 'up-ended'. When it was swimming, its pointed tail was slightly cocked, but now that it was dabbling with its head under water, its tail had fallen into line with its body, and stood up vertically. It was facing away from me, and I could see the distinctive black under the tail.

Some of these roaming drakes have a mate with them, but this one seemed to be alone. The female is not so easy to recognize – she does not have a noticeably long tail, and is like a slender, grey female mallard.

Pintails have a very sensitive tip to their beak, and can detect underwater worms and small aquatic snails when they 'up-end', but they do not dive like the tufted ducks. I watched my bird tip up and down several times.

Then something evidently disturbed it. It swam along with its tail lowered, like an uneasy dog. The shovelers went on shovelling, not far away – clearly they were thicker-skinned than the pintail.

Suddenly it was up in the air. It flew rapidly towards me, then swerved off. I could see its slim, streamlined shape in the sky, and I could even hear its wings hissing. It was soon out of sight – a winter wanderer that had gone in search of tranquillity.

I am not a natural twitcher. I would far rather stumble across a moderately uncommon bird, like a wryneck, for myself than stand on a crowded beach, hemmed in by telescopes like small cannons, and prams full of cameras, trying to see the first Forster's tern from America recorded for years.

However, two or three bitterns have been coming back every winter recently to a reed-bed just outside a hide near Cheshunt, in the Lea valley north of London. They are birds that one very rarely gets a good view of. In Norfolk and Suffolk, the only counties where they still breed, people hear their booming call echoing round the reed-beds on a summer's evening, but are lucky to get more than a glimpse of one suddenly flying by on owl-like wings and dropping into the impenetrable reeds again.

So I went to the hide last week. It was full of people who fell into two distinct categories – those who could see a bittern in the reeds just in front of them and those who couldn't. The ones who could were looking intently through the viewing slots with their field-glasses saying: 'There, there – by those three bent reeds, crouching very low – you can just see the barring on the flanks.'

'Where, where?' the others were saying with an air of anguish.

The bird was certainly well camouflaged. I couldn't detect it at first. Then one of the reeds shook slightly and I got it. In fact it was just about to move, and I saw it stalk a few feet through the water, a shadowy, hunchbacked shape.

It stopped again in a thick clump of reeds and went motionless. But by now I had it. I could make out its long beak, its gleaming eye, its dark crown – more blue than black, it seemed to me, though it is always described as black – its flecked breast and barred body. Once or twice it turned its head slowly; once, perhaps hearing a noise from the hide, it looked straight at us, opened its beak and hissed slightly.

I tried to pick out a distinctive piece of vegetation near it so that I could find it again if I took my glasses off it. But a dark reed-leaf that is very obvious through the glasses vanishes without them. The bittern was quite invisible to the naked eye, though it was only four or five yards away, and I almost lost it. I did luckily, find it again, and eventually I found a long, dried-up nettle which proved a reliable guide-line to it.

The hide is called the Waverley hide. It is open to the public free at weekends from 10am–4pm, and when the bitterns are there is generally open on the other weekdays, but on those days there is a small charge payable to a warden who looks in from time to time. Maps and details from the Countryside Centre, Abbey Gardens, Waltham Abbey, Essex.

I have been examining robins on Christmas cards. There are still plenty of them looking out of the holly with beady eyes, and most of them are not badly painted. All the same, live robins are much more beautiful. The Christmas card artists rarely show the delicate blue line that frames the red breast, and often omit even the white plumage below it. In nature, that is conspicuous. If you look up at a robin singing directly over your head in a hawthorn, you might think it was a white-breasted bird.

Robins are singing all over Britain now, except on a few mountain tops and moors. In London, in lamplit gardens, they can be heard in the middle of the night. In fact, far more robins sing in the winter than in the summer. This is because they sing in order to defend a territory – and in winter the female robins take up territories and sing too. In spring, the male's song also becomes a wooing song, and the

Robin

females give up their independence and find a mate. If their winter territory was next to the male's, they bring him quite a slice of land too.

The song is very sweet and penetrating, but has its variations. Normally a long burst of clear, liquid notes is followed by a softer passage; then the robin draws breath and launches itself again into a heartfelt outcry. It sits in a very characteristic way when singing, rather upright.

When two robins are in conflict over a territorial border, they will sometimes sing fiercely at each other, interspersing salvos of song with loud, ticking calls. They also lift their heads, display their red throats and breasts, and sway from side to side. It is the sight of the intruder's red breast that angers the territory owner, and it is these signals from the owner's red breast that in turn help to drive the invader away.

However, the robins perceive all this in a very different fashion from us. In his classic book, *The Life of the Robin*, published 50 years ago during the war, David Lack described a fascinating experiment. If he put a stuffed robin, with its red breast painted brown, in a robin's territory, the stuffed bird was ignored. But if he hung a bunch of robin breast feathers in the territory, without the rest of the bird, it was attacked. Robins would appear to see just the significant parts of other robins, not the birds as wholes.

They have a hard time of it when there is deep snow on the ground, because they feed mainly on small insects that run about on the leaves. That is the time to feed them. They are probably such popular birds because they are so tame – which is another way of saying that they are bold in their exploitation of humans. When it is hard to find food on the ground, they will dance attendance on pheasants that are scratching up the leaf-litter, or on unseen moles that are throwing up their mounds of earth. From there it is only a short step to sitting on the handle of a gardener's spade. Back to the Christmas cards!

Birds, like humans, want a coffee-break in the middle of the morning. However, as they have been looking for food and eating it since dawn, they do not consume anything more in their few moments of leisure; they just sit and preen, or do nothing.

I was walking across a field in the winter sunshine one morning last week and could see a whole crowd of birds ahead of me in a solitary oak out in the middle. I was facing the low sun, so I worked my way along the field edge until the sun was almost behind me.

The birds were still there. It was just ten o'clock, and they were all taking it easy. There were 11 collared doves scattered about the bare boughs, looking very pearly in the bright, almost horizontal light. Several were preening, prodding their beaks into their shoulders or breast; the rest were motionless, except when one of them occasionally became curious about something it had seen and stretched out its long neck to take a look.

There were also two jackdaws sitting close to each other and shuffling about on the branch. I could see their pale-grey eyes gleaming. Three rooks sailed lazily through the air and landed on the topmost branches, and they, too, started preening. A black feather floated down.

A comfortable coffee-group, and I left them in peace.

Collared Dove

Hunger would soon be gnawing at them and they would all be back at work again on the ground. They would be working late, too. Birds need to line their stomachs well against the long, cold winter nights.

The field I was in was a piece of set-aside land, with old stubble visible in the rough grass. It was not long before I saw something I was especially looking for; something that everyone hopes set-aside land will encourage. There was a whirr of wings, and the air was suddenly full of silver. It was a flock of about 40 skylarks going up, the low sun glinting on their pale underwings.

These winter flocks of skylarks, probably visitors from the Continent, are a fine sight in the air. They go across the field in a wispy cloud that changes shape all the time, as if they were being blown about by the wind. Then they all circle, fly back towards you, and move off again. My flock did this several times, then disappeared into the distance.

Jackdaw

Now I was getting near a wood I know. It is well packed with hornbeams, with oaks and beeches rising above them, and brambles still green and sharp-thorned on the ground.

There were various trickling and ticking sounds coming from the wood. One was obviously a robin's call – that rather firm rippling note they produce when they do not like another robin coming near. Another, more abrasive, was a worried wren. But there was also a thin, very watery trickle: the winter alarm-call of the yellowhammer.

Yellowhammers are not usually thought of as woodland birds, but at this season, when they are feeding together in the fields, they often fly up high into the trees of an adjacent wood. I soon picked one out in the bare twigs, its head an astonishingly vivid yellow in the winter sunlight. Two more flew up from almost under my feet and joined it, their streaky, reddish-chestnut mantles almost as colourful as their heads.

But what was that bird in a low tree at the edge of the wood? It had leant forward to peck at something until it was almost upside down, and its wings were fluttering open to show a white rump. It straightened up to reveal the scarlet breast of a bullfinch, then flew off. I went to see what it had been so keen to eat. One of the bramble stems had climbed up nine or ten feet among the boughs, and a few withered blackberries were still hanging on it.

Winter fare, you might think; but a great treat for a bullfinch.